ORDER

OUT

OF

CHAOS

ORDER
OUT
OF
CHAOS

A Kidnap Negotiator's Guide to Influence and Persuasion

ORDER OUT OF CHAOS

Win Every Negotiation, Thrive in Adversity, and Become a World-Class Communicator

SCOTT WALKER

HARVARD BUSINESS REVIEW PRESS

BOSTON, MASSACHUSETTS

The web addresses referenced in this book were live and correct at the time of the book's publication but may be subject to change.

Library of Congress Cataloging-in-Publication Data

Names: Walker, Scott (Writer on negotiation), author.
Title: Order out of chaos : a kidnap negotiator's guide to influence and
    persuasion / Scott Walker.
Description: Boston, Massachusetts : Harvard Business Review Press,
    [2023] | Includes index.
Identifiers: LCCN 2023039631 (print) | LCCN 2023039632 (ebook) |
    ISBN 9781647827243 (hardcover) | ISBN 9781647827250 (epub)
Subjects: LCSH: Negotiation. | Communication—Psychological aspects. |
    Communication in management. | Emotional intelligence. | Conflict management.
Classification: LCC BF637.N4 W335 2023 (print) | LCC BF637.N4 (ebook) |
    DDC 158/.5—dc23/eng/20231201
LC record available at https://lccn.loc.gov/2023039631
LC ebook record available at https://lccn.loc.gov/2023039632

ISBN: 978-1-64782-724-3
eISBN: 978-1-64782-725-0

The paper used in this publication meets the requirements of the American National Standard for Permanence of Paper for Publications and Documents in Libraries and Archives Z39.48-1992.

Author's Note

The negotiation case studies in this book are all based on actual events. However, in order to protect those involved and to respect confidentiality, certain key details have been changed, including amalgamating cases where appropriate. Dialogue exchanges are not verbatim, nor should they be treated as such.

Dedicated to all of my "teachers," who have provided me with opportunities to walk the talk, fail often, and learn many lessons along the way.

This book is also dedicated to LH—SSTFILPG.
It's certainly been worth the wait.

Above all, to S and J; my love knows no bounds.

Contents

Preface

Life is a negotiation. Every single day you are negotiating, even if you're not actually saying anything. Because what is negotiation, if it isn't about one person attempting to influence or persuade another to think, feel, or act in a certain way, regardless of whether they are willing to or not? This applies to a coworker, your boss, neighbors, kids, spouse, or even the person working in your local store.

That is why this book teaches you how to become a world-class communicator and, in so doing, become the best negotiator you can be. Words matter, and being able to negotiate successfully with everyone you meet is about knowing how to communicate effectively. It is the most important skill you will ever learn.

Sometimes, how you negotiate can have serious implications if you misjudge what you say or how you say it. When you're feeling stressed or under pressure, the chances of this happening increase. As a kidnap negotiator, I know only too well what crisis and chaos looks, sounds, and feels like. Not only has being able to negotiate and communicate effectively saved my life and the lives of others on many occasions, it has also made me successful in business and, most importantly of all, a better and more fulfilled person.

Thankfully, few people will ever have to face a situation in which a hostile kidnapper is threatening to execute a hostage, but my hope is that by teaching you the proven tools of successful crisis negotiation, this book will transform your life, both personally and professionally. While the material contained in this book is built on decades of extensive scientific and academic research, it has also been forged in real-world application where the stakes simply can't get any higher.

In this book, you will learn essential negotiation principles, strategies, tools, and techniques, supported by real-life case studies that you can begin applying immediately. Add them to your repertoire and watch not just your mastery of negotiation but also your communication skills improve when they matter most.

Mastering a Negotiator's Mindset

Chapter 1 introduces the foundations to being a successful negotiator and world-class communicator, which begins in the mind. Success in any endeavor is based primarily on your mindset and psychology, with less on how you achieve it. You'll learn powerful tools to develop a winning mindset that will enable you to master resilient emotional self-regulation and remain grounded and centered amid crises, conflict, and uncertainty. You will also learn how to increase your emotional intelligence capacity, which will, in turn, improve your communication and awareness of yourself and others exponentially.

Preparing to Win Every Negotiation

Chapter 2 teaches you a three-step process that prepares you to triumph in any negotiation. Learn how to take things in your stride with focus, clarity, and calmness, regardless of how overwhelming the circumstances may be. Develop your own powerful Immediate Action drill to extract yourself from situations in which you find yourself hijacked emotionally and needing to rescue the deal. We'll also look at ways of ensuring long-term negotiation success by surrounding yourself with a winning team and how to establish a robust yet agile working routine over an extended period of time.

Practical Psychology to Influence Any Negotiation

Chapter 3 draws back the curtain on negotiation psychology and challenges outdated thinking and research on how our brains work and their impact on our emotions. Learn the easy-to-apply yet powerful Jedi-mind tricks that will take your negotiations to the next level. Develop a deeper understanding of a proven, evidence-based negotiation framework within which you can take regular, meaningful action and apply techniques to influence and persuade anyone on anything, at any time.

Avoiding Common Negotiation Mistakes

Chapter 4 offers ways to spot and avoid the most common negotiation mistakes people make. You'll learn how to identify both your personal barriers to effective communication that often arise subconsciously as well as those entrenched organizational blocks that are often found in the systems, processes, and culture of an organization. We'll cover how to embrace communication conflict in a healthy way that allows you to keep your cool and still achieve negotiation success. In doing so, we'll also discover how to defuse and overcome any negativity or challenge others may levy against you or your proposal.

Negotiating with Difficult People

Chapter 5 brings together all the tools and techniques from the previous chapters. It teaches you how to succeed in conversations with "difficult" people. You'll learn how to plan for such conversations and uncover the reasons why they might be difficult in the first place. Learn how to identify what their real and unspoken needs are that must to be met before you can succeed. The book concludes by showing you how to identify and mitigate any risks that might impact your negotiation.

Introduction

I always wanted to be a cop: not a uniformed bobby on the beat, but a detective, solving crimes and putting villains behind bars. And, for sixteen years, I did just that. I threw myself into investigating everything, from petty shoplifting to murder and terrorism, and I loved every minute.

One afternoon, I was sitting in the canteen at the Greenwich police station in London, catching up with a colleague. He looked exhausted, but was full of professional pride as he took me through the four days he'd just spent in something called a Red Center, helping to resolve the kidnapping of a drug dealer by a rival Albanian gang. I was hooked and hanging on to his every word, even though I didn't understand all of it. It was a long way from the overflowing inbox of crime reports I needed to process before the day was out.

"You should give it a go," he said and offered to introduce me to the Hostage Crisis and Negotiation Unit (HCNU), based at Scotland Yard, who are responsible for training both UK and international police officers, as well as members of the military, in the art of negotiation. I already knew of their world-class reputation, alongside those of their FBI and New York Police Department counterparts. At the time, the HCNU also managed the on-call roster for officers willing to take on the additional responsibility of having their private lives interrupted at the most inconvenient moments, as they raced across London to help negotiate the release of people who had been kidnapped. I took him up on the offer of the introduction; I was subsequently selected and, for the next few years, I fully immersed myself in this unique world as I watched and learned from the very best.

In 2015, I left the police force and continued to build my experience in kidnap-for-ransom negotiations and other similar perils, as what's called a *response consultant*. Such is the prevalence of these crimes that, since then, I've had the opportunity to help resolve hundreds of cases all over the world.

By way of definition, *crisis negotiation* usually refers to the type of incident where somebody is standing on the ledge of a tall building threatening to jump off. A *hostage negotiation* might involve a bank robbery that has gone wrong, perhaps leaving the criminals holed up inside with members of the public and staff. This is particularly so within a law enforcement setting, as it is usually police officers who will attempt to resolve these types of incidents. *Kidnap-for-ransom negotiations* usually refer to situations in which somebody has been taken by force and a concession (usually money) is being demanded for their release.

Outside of law enforcement, the terms *kidnap* and *hostage negotiations* are often used interchangeably to describe this latter scenario, and there are a small number of highly trained private individuals who perform this role. I was told on my selection course that more people have been to the International Space Station than operate as highly trained, full-time professional response consultants.

For the next few years, this is what I did, always keeping my equipment bag with me and staying no more than three hours away from a major airport. The high tempo of the work meant that during this period, I helped resolve more than three hundred cases of kidnapping and other similar crises, such as piracy, extortion, and cyberattack. These negotiations occurred all over the world, from the United Kingdom, the United States, Canada, Europe, and the Middle East to India, Singapore, the Philippines, Australia, China, Africa, and Latin America.

Over time, I was able to identify which patterns worked and which didn't, and in the process I developed a unique understanding of what makes people think, feel, and act the way they do. What I found so striking when I started working with business leaders is the sheer amount of crossover between business and kidnap negotiations. So much of what works in the latter can be successfully applied to the former. In fact, these similarities show up in any difficult conversation, the sort you may be putting off because you anticipate it will result in high levels of tension or emotion.

Successfully resolving a kidnapping or business negotiation with ease and wise care uses the same skills as those required in any stressful conversation. This dexterity can also be used to influence and persuade others without necessarily having the authority that comes from holding senior rank or a fancy job title.

The situations I've faced are just extreme versions of everyday events, such as placating an ego-driven boss, negotiating a pay raise, having that difficult conversation you've been putting off, or even getting your teenager to do as they're told. These scenarios all require deep and empathetic listening, meeting the needs of others, managing expectations, and overcoming obstacles.

My role in any kidnap-for-ransom negotiation was to bring stability, calm, discipline, and, ultimately, order out of chaos. This could only be achieved by using finely tuned and highly effective communication with people from a wide range of backgrounds, all with wildly different cultures, values, beliefs, and goals. Luckily, to achieve this, it wasn't necessary for me to invent some magic Jedi-mind trick or develop an effective strategy for influencing and persuading people all by myself. Like most successful people, regardless of their field, experience, or high levels of ability, I stand on the shoulders of many giants who have gone before me.

It is easier to do this work if you are curious and can tap into a focused and agile mindset. Success is also more likely if you try to do your best with what is often referred to as a "beginner's mind"—treating every situation as if you were encountering it for the first time. I also watched, listened, and learned from other negotiator colleagues, seeking to absorb their wisdom. Even the most experienced negotiator will have the humility to reach out to others for suggestions when facing a seemingly intractable problem while deployed in some far-off, dusty place. Emulating their example enabled me to avoid the trap of unconscious bias, flawed decision-making, and habitual thought patterns.

While learning from colleagues, I also witnessed some exemplary communication and impressive mindsets among my clients, no matter whether they were heading up a family-run startup, an important government department, or one of the biggest corporations on the planet. And then there were the hostages themselves and their families. Their ability to regulate their own emotions, stay grounded, and communicate with confidence inspired everyone around them. I have condensed into this book everything I observed, processed, and successfully applied in real-life cases over ten years.

My ultimate goal was to consistently influence and persuade other people to follow a certain course of action, particularly when they didn't want to. I wasn't driven by some Machiavellian intent to manipulate, but rather out of sheer necessity. It wasn't as if I could just walk away and leave the hostages to their fate when kidnappers didn't play nice or a cyber-extortionist had encrypted a hospital's computer network and the risk to the health of thousands of patients was increasing with each passing second.

The desired outcome would only ever happen once I'd managed to do one thing: connect with the bad guy on a human level. This meant displaying huge amounts of genuine empathy toward that person, so they felt truly seen, heard, and understood. They needed to feel that I considered their own perspective or unique "model of the world" as valid as anyone else's, even if I didn't agree with them or share their viewpoint or methods, which I never did. That didn't matter, though. Because therein lies the golden rule of effective negotiation—*it's not about you*. If I'd allowed the unhealthy aspects of either my ego or those of the hostage's family or organization to be in the driver's seat, it would've caused a breakdown in communication, resulting in tragedy; and, on occasion, it almost did.

A case highlighting this involved the eldest brother of a wealthy family, who had been kidnapped with a ransom demand of over $10 million. The hostage's younger brother, because of the language barrier, assumed the role of the negotiator or "communicator" with the kidnappers. Despite the family's ability to pay the vast sums of money demanded, thankfully they took the advice not to pay it, as it would only encourage the kidnappers to hold out for even more money and place other family members at risk in the future.

Understandably, the younger brother was deeply angry and upset with what had happened to his sibling and didn't hold back from voicing his frustrations with the kidnappers whenever they made contact. Ignoring our advice, he eventually allowed his ego to get the better of him and went too far. Nothing was heard from the kidnappers for several months, creating untold anxiety for the family. Eventually, we managed to persuade the brother to step down and hand this vital communication role to a calmer family member who was able to master their emotions and put judgment and blame for what had happened to one side. The hostage was released a couple of months later.

Being able to negotiate effectively is vital, whoever you are and whatever your role in life. And while doing so may seem simple, it is certainly far from easy. Sending a message, whether verbally, physically, or electronically, is only half of the equation. For the communication to be truly effective, the receiver has to interpret it in exactly the way you intended them to, otherwise there is a mismatch and the potential for a negotiation breakdown occurs.

Not only do words matter, but how you say them is just as crucial. The language you use creates the meaning for every single situation and circumstance you find yourself in, as you react and respond to the words and behavior of other people. To negotiate with a genuine open awareness and curiosity—without shame, blame, or judgment—is not easy. Yet to do so is a superpower that you can develop over time and with regular practice. Developing such mastery is crucial if you want to achieve success in any area of life.

For me to be judgmental about the kidnappers in the middle of a negotiation might be considered a natural and reasonable response, especially if they threaten to kill or torture the hostages or even enact a mock execution over the telephone to their families or colleagues, causing untold distress and suffering. Yet for me to stay anything other than calm, objective, and empathetic would be counterproductive. The kidnappers, just like every other person alive, simply want to feel like they matter, that their needs and concerns are valid. It's just that their methods of achieving that are highly questionable.

It's not about letting them "get away with it" or being bullied into submission. Nor is it about giving them what they initially demanded. Far from it, in fact. Being laser-focused on my outcome—the safe and timely release of the hostages—means I can keep aspects of my ego in check and use my negotiation skills to validate the kidnappers' model of the world, persuade them to significantly reduce their demands, and ultimately release the hostages completely unharmed.

This approach applies in any form of negotiation. Remember, you're negotiating every single day, even when you don't realize it: dealing with difficult situations where you have to influence and persuade someone else to give you what you want, whether you're looking to close that elusive business deal, planning a family holiday, or even making your significant other know that they're the only person in the world who really matters to you.

In fact, you are always negotiating, from the words you use and the tone of your delivery to the subtle changes in your facial expressions and the way you sit, stand, or move. Even by doing or saying nothing, you are negotiating. Recognizing this enables you to increase your ability to negotiate effectively while understanding its impact on yourself and others.

It's also worth remembering that you don't just want to think about negotiating effectively with the person on the *other* side of the table; you also need to be able to do so with colleagues and other people who are supporting you on *your* side. This can sometimes be more challenging than those you're "officially" negotiating with because ego, game-playing, and office politics can all get in the way. This is called the "crisis within the crisis," and it's far more common than you realize. During a kidnapping case, typically at least 80 percent of my time was spent focused on client management, with the remaining 20 percent on the actual negotiation with the kidnappers.

This "crisis within a crisis" can be seen in organizations all over the world. There isn't an industry or sector that is immune. In my experience, the individuals, teams, and departments who compete against each other within the same company—rather than channeling all of that time, energy, and focus into working collaboratively in the interests of their clients and customers—have forgotten that there is enough of the pie for everyone to have dessert. This is not about avoiding healthy and friendly competition to see who can sell the best product or service. Instead, it's about creating an environment that enables honest, direct negotiation while avoiding a toxic, unforgiving culture.

This internal dog-eat-dog mentality is indicative of leaders who are driven by the primary emotions of fear and anger, who are led by their ego and a need to control and assert their authority and dominance. This is not the same as being hungry for success, wanting to dominate their industry, or pushing for extreme competitive advantage, which are fundamental to business growth.

Ultimately, this book will transform how you lead your team, run your business, interact with your family or community, and ultimately, how successfully you live your life. You may be an executive in a multinational organization, the owner of a small business, a local sports team coach, or running the family household. Thankfully, while it is highly unlikely that you will ever have to use these skills to resolve a real-life kidnapping or hostage situation, the principles and techniques covered in this book will help you navigate the pitfalls and common mistakes people make and give you the confidence to succeed every time.

I now train these proven and powerful negotiation techniques to leaders and teams at all levels of an organization who are keen to enhance their resilience and emotional intelligence, along with their negotiation and sales skills. These skills allow them to become the calm center of any storm and bring order out of chaos, achieving whatever business goals they set their mind to. All of this is crucial during these times of crisis and significant change.

I also particularly enjoy designing and facilitating immersive tabletop exercises for clients based on real kidnap cases to upskill individuals and teams in leadership, decision-making, and negotiation skills under extreme, life-or-death pressure. It never fails to impress me how many people who might be overlooked or not considered naturally suited to these roles flourish under such high-pressure circumstances, taking themselves and their colleagues by surprise.

Conversely, the opposite is also true. I've lost count how many times an ego-driven leader with low sensory acuity has blundered their way through the initial stages before freezing when I suddenly hand them the phone with an irate "kidnapper" (played by an actor) doing everything to trigger and undermine them.

The leaders who learn from these scenarios and apply the techniques that you're going to be taught in this book go on to develop and empower some of the most productive and high-performing teams I've ever seen, achieving exponential success as a result. This is not because what I teach is some kind of magic. Instead, it is thanks to the consistent application of the fundamentals of effective negotiation, which work every time. None of this can truly be mastered, though, without the following principle being etched into your brains whenever you're engaged in any form of communication and, particularly, in any negotiation: *first seek to understand, before being understood.*

ORDER
OUT
OF
CHAOS

ORDER

OUT

OF

CHAOS

CHAPTER ONE

Mastering a Negotiator's Mindset

I t is fair to say that we are all living in a volatile, uncertain, complex, and ambiguous time. In recent years, our society has faced significant challenges, ranging from climate change, inequality, racial tension, and a global pandemic to war between countries close to home and a huge rise in the cost of living. As a result, people are struggling with the debilitating effects of overwhelming stress and cognitive clutter that pervade their daily lives and put their mental health under strain.

If you were being totally honest, you would probably acknowledge that you sometimes find yourself being taken hostage (metaphorically, at least) by these effects, often by simply watching the news or scrolling through social media until you find something that triggers you—usually something outside of your control, in any event. Perhaps you find yourself adding fuel to the fire by posting a comment online about the offending article before mulling it over and over in your mind, thereby compounding your frustration and sense of suffering. More often than not, you allow yourself to become hostage to your own disempowering mindset.

These days, it seems everyone is shouting, but no one is listening to other people's viewpoints. There has never been a more pressing need for you to improve your negotiation and leadership skills to help guide not only yourself but also your people through these challenging times. It seems that, as a society, we are starved of better conversations—in our teams, across our organizations, in our communities, and with our families. If you can acknowledge this and give it the space it needs to be truly absorbed, then maybe you can acknowledge and satiate a real hunger to first have better conversations with yourself. Only by doing so will you be able to improve your mindset and the mindset and mental well-being of others, transforming both your personal and professional lives in the process.

In this chapter, I will share with you three key techniques that are crucial to developing a powerful mindset, capable of communicating and negotiating effectively regardless of the circumstances.

Technique 1: Creating order out of chaos: Harnessing your Red Center

Technique 2: Taking control of your internal state

Technique 3: Developing emotional intelligence to improve your negotiation skills

But first . . .

• • •

Negotiation Case File #1: Middle East and Asia

From the many conversations and debriefs I've conducted with former hostages, what is striking is that the ones who not only survived, but came out the least damaged by their experience, had developed a positive mindset.

While they were held captive, these hostages firmly placed their focus and attention on what was happening in their mind. Rather than stepping into a spiral of despair and labeling themselves as a victim, in a pejorative sense, they took control of how they responded and ultimately reframed their experience into a positive one from which they could grow, share, develop, and learn. Such a mindset is exemplified in William Ernest Henley's poem "Invictus." In it, Henley advocates that no matter how difficult or painful the circumstances, we are all "masters of our fate" and "captains of our soul." In other words, we get to control the narrative inside our own mind.

It's December 1966. A US naval A-4 Skyhawk fighter jet from the aircraft carrier USS *Kitty Hawk* is flying thousands of feet over North Vietnam. Eleven years of fighting has devastated the land, which is clearly evident from the cockpit of the Skyhawk. But the pilot, Dan Glenn, has far more pressing things on his mind, as his plane has just been shot by the Vietnamese. With no hope of making it back, Glenn reaches for the ejector handle and braces himself for the double-figure g-force that is about to rip through his body.

As soon as his parachute touches down on the rice field, local villagers surround and strip him before parading him through their village. The next day, he is blindfolded and handcuffed and taken on a slow six-day trek to the Hoa Lo Prison, sardonically referred to as the "Hanoi Hilton." He is unaware at this point that he will spend more than half of his 2,265 days as a prisoner of war there, nor that he will be regularly subjected to solitary confinement, torture, and extreme interrogation.

Glenn is aware, however, that while he cannot control the torture, he can control what he focuses on and what meaning he gives to his experience. Glenn and his fellow prisoners purposefully focused on something, anything, other than feeling pity for themselves for the situation they are in. For example, they devised a tap code to communicate with each other through the prison's thick walls, consisting of different noises to represent certain letters and words, some to warn if a guard was nearby. Even more impressively, Glenn spent his time in solitary confinement designing and building his dream house in fine detail, all in his mind, which he went on to successfully build and live in upon his release, many years later.

Glenn isn't alone in his thinking. In 1987, as an envoy for the Church of England, Terry Waite traveled to Lebanon to try to secure the release of four hostages but was himself kidnapped and held captive until his release in 1991. Of his 1,763 days in captivity, four years were spent in total and complete isolation, neither seeing nor speaking to another soul except a few cursory words with his guards when they brought him food. In an interview after he was released, Waite describes how he was chained up for twenty-three hours and fifty minutes a day. He used this time to write his first book, *Taken on Trust*, in his head as he had nothing to write with or on. He attributes this to keeping him mentally alive throughout his ordeal.

Waite firmly believed that while his captors might have had the power to break his body, "My soul is not yours to possess." He was also pragmatic, without a false sense of naive positivity. He knew he might very easily die in prison, but he kept telling himself, "Don't give way to morbid thoughts. You still have life today."

* * *

In more recent times, the Gulf of Guinea off the west coast of Africa has been a notorious spot for piracy, or *maritime kidnappings*, as they are known—so much so that maritime kidnappings in this region account for 95 percent of all crew members abducted from ships globally. Whereas pirates operating in the early years of the twenty-first century off Somalia on the east coast of Africa used to take the ship as well as the crew, they now storm the ship and take a few crew members at gunpoint, leaving the rest on board to continue on their way. This type of attack has become so pervasive that there is hardly a professional kidnap response consultant in the business who hasn't negotiated a case like this in West Africa.

On one such negotiation a few years ago, following a ransom payment and safe release of all the crew, I was one of the first people to speak with them as part of the debrief process. Even though none of the crew had even heard of Dan Glenn or Terry Waite, the ones who had survived their ordeal in the best possible shape were the ones who had applied a similar mindset to them.

When I asked about how they had coped, they were very matter-of-fact in their response, as if it were somehow second nature to them. Some were convinced that either their families or the company would eventually work out a way to get them released, even if they had no way of knowing whether that would be in days, weeks, months, or even years. In the meantime, they would focus on whatever they could control and avoid worrying about anything else.

Some planned in minute detail the family holidays they would take or the business they would set up upon their release. Others just took one moment at a time, without worrying about the past or being anxious about what might or might not happen in the future. This didn't mean that any of these hostages were naive or failed to confront the most brutal facts of their current reality, but they knew the importance of seeing the situation for what it was and accepting that "this too shall pass."

Utilizing such a mindset is not reserved only for those people who find themselves in extreme life-or-death hardships. Instead, it can be used by all of us who, with consistent practice, can also improve our mindset and, in turn, our communication and leadership skills in everyday life.

If you're about to embark on a delicate business negotiation with a client, for example, it is your responsibility to set out with the right mindset and tone, bringing more curiosity than assumptions to the table. Or when you make a mistake, you may decide to embrace and learn from what might be difficult feedback to hear from your boss or colleagues.

Engaging in this level of negotiation with yourself is like going to the gym and building muscle; you need to work at it *all the time*. So, every day, stand guard at the door of your mind, because, remember, *you* control the story.

Technique 1: Creating Order out of Chaos: Harnessing Your Red Center

By its very nature, the physical kidnapping of another human being tends to be violent and sudden. The immediate aftermath is often confusing for the relatives and colleagues of the hostage as they face almost overwhelming levels of uncertainty and fear. These are the very two things kidnappers will exploit to extract as much money as possible, while sowing seeds of doubt and distrust—the epitome of chaos. Without discipline, focus, and a clear strategy imposed on the negotiation, people could die.

My job as a kidnap negotiator was to bring calm and order to this chaos so that I could ensure everyone got out alive and the crisis was resolved swiftly and effectively. I was able to do this only by identifying and harnessing my Red Center.

What is a Red Center?

In the kidnap industry, particularly within law enforcement, the term *Red Center* is ordinarily used to describe the epicenter of the negotiation and refers to the physical location—usually a room in a house, hotel, or office—where the family member or colleague of the hostage is receiving phone calls and demands from the kidnappers. It is a chaotic place, full of highly charged emotion, where people's lives hang in the balance.

If you're expecting it to be full of highly sophisticated technology, with wall-to-wall monitors beaming live images from satellites, tracking every move of the kidnappers—like in the movies—then I'm sorry to disappoint you.

In one case, I met with the brother of a hostage who had begun receiving calls from the kidnappers. A colleague and I then took him to a central London hotel, where we used one of their suites to establish a Red Center, as the case had all the hallmarks of running for a while. As we walked in, the brother stopped in the doorway.

"You're kidding me, right?" he snarled.

"What do you mean?" I asked.

"Where's all the equipment? You know, the monitors and stuff?"

I laughed and sat down on one of the sofas, pulling out three items from my pocket, arranging them neatly on the glass coffee table in front of me.

"These are going to get your brother back, not some fancy gear and satellite feeds," I said, pointing to the pen, notepad, and small recording device in front of me.

"Now, sit down and let's prepare what you're going to say when they call next."

What I didn't tell him was that in the background, on the other side of London, a lot of resources were being thrown at this case, just like in the latest blockbuster action movie. In most Western countries, law enforcement agencies usually go to extreme lengths to identify who and where the kidnappers are before storming their stronghold, rescuing the hostages, and arresting the bad guys. But none of this works unless two human beings can communicate with one another to reach an agreement.

Unfortunately, not all countries have such highly trained and professional police or military units, and such a tactical option is usually avoided in more challenging and unstable parts of the world. This is particularly so when it might be the police or military who are involved in the actual kidnapping or are complicit in some way. In these cases, a negotiated settlement provides the best odds of success. There is a more than 90 percent chance of the hostages being released and safely returned to their loved ones through a structured negotiation process that uses sound and proven psychological techniques. The small minority of hostages who, sadly, don't make it home alive usually die because either they were injured in the initial abduction and later died of their wounds, or they were killed in attempting to escape or in a failed hostage rescue attempt.

Ultimately, negotiations in a kidnapping should be seen as a simple business negotiation. While this might be unpalatable to some, particularly to families of the hostages, to do otherwise is to increase the risk by allowing negative emotions to cloud the decision-making and negotiation process. One of the most important actions I'll take at the start of a case is to sit down with the hostage's family or the organization's senior leadership team and explain my suggested strategy, along with its pros and cons, as nothing in these negotiations is without significant risk. We're not operating in a world of absolute certainties or guarantees.

Regardless of where in the world the negotiation is taking place, kidnappings are not usually resolved by technology alone, but by highly effective communication between one person and another, back and forth, until a deal is struck. This is only possible if you can manage your emotional state and keep a level head when everyone else is losing theirs. It's about staying focused and seeing it through to a successful outcome, regardless of how challenging and scary the journey might be.

As I became more experienced, I came to realize that the concept of a Red Center is not just useful in a hostage negotiation. It's a place deep within all of us we can tap into when we're faced with unexpected or unpleasant situations. It is also a place where you can strip back the fear and unhelpful conditioning built up over a lifetime that gets in the way of you achieving your full potential. The techniques in this book form the basis of creating such a Red Center, which you can refine and adapt for yourself.

Why is it important?

In a kidnap negotiation, emotions understandably run high, ranging from boredom and apathy through to fear and elation. As the negotiator in the middle of it all, attempting to corral, inspire, advise, and facilitate requires a finely tuned sensory acuity. It's being able to pick up on the subtle shifts in mood and emotions of the crisis management team (CMT), the hostage's family, the communicator, the kidnappers, and, most of all, myself.

Each day I was on a case, I would wake up and take a reading of how I was feeling by tuning into my own built-in emotional barometer, my Red Center. When I was deployed on the ground, rather than remotely managing the situation over the phone from thousands of miles away, doing this emotional check-in was even more important.

Just imagine if I turned up at the client's offices, camp, or embassy before a day's tough negotiations and was miserable and frustrated. How well do you think that would've gone down? Just how calm, rational, and objective would I have been in the midst of extreme threats and pressure tactics? Ultimately, I owed it to the hostages and their families to show up every single day grounded, switched on, and focused with an agile mind, rather than being fear-driven, rigid, and a control freak, which often shows up in people when they find themselves outside their comfort zone or their threshold of control.

Consider asking yourself the following questions:

- How can you set yourself up for success and show up every day as your best version, even when you don't feel like it?

- What needs to happen for you to follow through and even enjoy the process?

- What obstacles are likely to get in your way of doing this?

You may not be negotiating with kidnappers, but using the techniques described in this book to create your own Red Center will reap rewards for you in both your personal and professional lives. What a Red Center will do is enable you to meet adversity head-on and think, negotiate, and decide far more effectively than before. It will help you to crush that important business deal, study for a degree while holding down two jobs, run your first 10K race, lose stubborn post-holiday weight, or achieve that long-held dream, whatever that might be for you.

Applying the strategies in this book will also enable you to identify and overcome your fears, turning indecision into confident action, all while having better conversations with your teams, clients, families, and, ultimately, yourself.

Exercise

One way you can manage your emotional state and harness your Red Center is by using this simple three-step process, which will enable you to take everything in your stride, specifically in moments of uncertainty and confusion. It will support you to make effective decisions while you are leading yourself and others.

First, *acknowledge* and *accept* where you find yourself in that very moment. Take ownership. Second, locate where in your *body* you are experiencing the tension, tightness, or some other uncomfortable feeling. Third, *breathe* through that sensation, sitting with it, not forcing it away or allowing yourself to be consumed by it. Step into it—see, feel, and experience it—until it begins to dissipate. Clinging to the sensation or trying to force it away, however unpleasant it may be, will only increase the duration and intensity of the uncomfortable feeling.

Only once you've taken these steps can you begin to *clarify* what triggered you in the first place. Consider what is it that you need to work on (*hint:* it's usually something within yourself) to enable you to operate, interact, and decide from a place of strength rather than with a knee-jerk or ill-considered reaction or opinion.

By moving through these stages, you'll begin to embody feelings of calmness, highly tuned intuition, and presence, which will allow you to negotiate far more effectively.

Technique 2: Taking Control of Your Internal State

The world's best communicators know only too well the importance of having the right mindset to succeed in any form of negotiation. It's the one skill set that underpins literally everything, whether negotiating a business deal, your kid's bedtime, or persuading your partner where to go on holiday. The most powerful way to develop a strong mindset is through managing your own emotions, as all of your experiences in life are determined by the quality of the emotional state you are in at that particular time.

What do we mean by "state," and how can we control it?

State is everything. It is simply the emotional feeling you have 24/7/365. It covers anything from frustration, disappointment, anger, jealousy, and depression all the way through to joy, happiness, fulfillment, peace, determination, curiosity, certainty, confidence. When you're in the right state, it enables you to think, feel, and act with greater clarity, focus, and purpose. Emotion can also be viewed as energy or even as energy in motion. Experiencing and managing heightened levels of emotion (positive or negative) can be used as fuel to propel you through any challenge or obstacle you may face, particularly when it comes to negotiation.

Emotional mastery and regulation are the foundations of all success

As a professional negotiator, being able to master and regulate my emotions can be a matter of life or death. If I overreact or allow my ego to get in the way, it only increases the risks to the hostages. This level of mastery is also applicable to daily life. Think about it for a moment. You might be enjoying success as a corporate executive, business owner, stay-at-home parent, or sports team coach, but if your primary emotion is one of frustration, anger, or insecurity, then that will dictate not only your behavior, but also the quality of your life, irrespective of how much money you have in the bank or the fancy cars on your driveway.

How you negotiate with yourself is crucial. In fact, those conversations are probably the most important ones you'll ever have. Achieving the result you're looking for, whether that's a pay raise, a business deal, or training to run your first marathon, depends on whether you negotiate with yourself using empowering and positive language or the disempowering and negative kind. It is often said that you wouldn't talk to your worst enemies the way you might speak to yourself. Research has found that the quality of your self-talk can actually change the way you see yourself, your very identity, and therefore how you behave. Common negative self-talk usually involves a version of, "I'm not qualified or good enough," "I've got it wrong again," or even, "I'll never be able to achieve x."

The good news is, your brain is highly malleable and is open to changing the way you think, feel, and act, particularly when it comes to language and the meaning you give things. So these negative comments, along with the significance you've given them, can be overcome and replaced by far more empowering affirmations, such as, "I've got this," "I know what I'm doing and feel so passionate about it," "I've earned this," or "I am worthy and more than enough." Like all effective techniques, though, this is not a onetime checklist exercise, after which everything will be fine. It requires regular effort, as small steps consistently applied equal sustained success.

Managing your state in everyday life

Emotions shape and control the quality of your life, yet not as you might think. If a business deal you've been working hard on doesn't go through or you lose your car keys, you're likely to experience an emotion and then react in a certain way. As you now know, that emotion and subsequent action depend on the meaning or interpretation you give the situation. For example, you might say to yourself, "I can't get anything right. I'm always doing this," versus saying, "It's just one of those things. No worries. What can I learn from this?" The meaning or interpretation you've given the event is based on your unique and characteristic way of seeing the world. As the ancient Stoic philosopher Epictetus said, "Men are disturbed not by things, but by the view which they take of them." Managing your own emotional and psychological state of mind is crucial not just to negotiate the release of a hostage, but for success in life generally.

In the case of parenting, for example, the psychologist and best-selling author of several books on raising children Dr. Shefali Tsabary argues that when parents find themselves triggered by the child's behavior, they should try to focus on understanding what the triggers might mean. With the understanding that the child's behavior is merely trying to tell the parent something the child is unable to communicate effectively, the parent can then begin to change the pattern of how they respond to the behavior.

Once they feel like their parent understands them, the child is more likely to change their behavior. As a parent of teenagers, I know only too well how simple this sounds, yet it is not so easy to consistently implement. But trust me, it's worth the effort.

One way of viewing such an exchange is that all communication can be classed as either a "cry for help" or a "loving response." So next time you're engaged in an emotive communication, consider which one of these bests describes the words or behavior of the other person (as well as yourself).

HOW YOU FEEL	YOUR CHILD'S NEED
Annoyed	Attention
Challenged	Some form of "control" or decision-making
Hurt, in response to child saying, "I hate you," etc.	Revenge. Child is really saying, "Help me. I'm feeling unloved."

Thankfully, most people will never find themselves negotiating the release of a loved one who's been taken hostage. Nevertheless, you will still get lots of opportunity to practice the tools, tactics, and concepts in this book in your daily life, specifically in managing your state, as the world is full of things that will trigger you.

It could be when somebody does or says something you don't like or maybe doesn't do or say something you want them to. You may be caught in a traffic jam, experience a sudden increase in taxes, or hear the latest utterances of your least-favorite politician. You can fill in your own favorite flavor of suffering here. As the author, speaker, and trauma therapist Gabor Maté acknowledges, whenever we are emotionally triggered, somebody else may pull that trigger, but we are the ones carrying the ammunition inside us that causes us to react the way we do.

Recognizing an emotion in response to a trigger is also where, in the midst of communicating with another person, you can learn to harness the very moment between that experience and what you subsequently say or do as a direct result. No matter the ordeal you're facing or how insurmountable the odds, you are far more resilient and capable of managing your emotions than you may at first believe.

You may think you have lots of influence over situations or other people, yet the only thing you really control is the meaning—the story—you give something and, therefore, your response, rather than simply your reaction. This meaning or story is, in turn, like a lens through which you create your identity and how you see yourself in the world. It also influences how you view your position in every negotiation you engage in. For example, do you feel inferior, superior, or perhaps equal to the other person? The answer to this will dictate how you show up and communicate in any given scenario. Even in times of crisis, conflict, or significant change, you still get to control the meaning and response.

Park that ego

In any situation requiring strong communication, but particularly in a crisis, there is no room for ego. The most effective negotiators realize this and park theirs at the door. They understand the necessity of being able to manage their thoughts and behavior effectively. This equally applies whether you are the CEO of a global corporation facing a significant threat to the viability or reputation of your business or a stay-at-home parent.

Nor do the world's best negotiators seek to play the hero either, despite most crises providing the opportunity to do so. The Latin root of the word *hero* translates as "protect" or "serve." This kind of mindset underpins the number-one rule of being a world-class negotiator: *it's not about you.* It's always about the other side, which is why we must first seek to understand before being understood.

While you will have your own desired outcomes for each communication you engage in—as well as red lines that must not be crossed—the moment you actively listen and go out of your way to make the other person feel safe, seen, heard, and understood, it becomes a game changer. This way, you're also more likely to get what you want. In a business context, you don't just want it to be a onetime transaction, where they agree to this deal but didn't particularly like the way you achieved it, so they won't be coming back for a second one. You want to create raving fan clients, customers, and colleagues who can't wait to do business with you again because of how you treated them and made them feel.

The alternative is remaining locked in some form of gladiatorial battle of, "My position is more right and important than yours." Accepting another person's position is not naive or weak but comes instead from a place of working toward achieving an end goal, outcome, or mission for the team or organization, all while showing empathy and compassion through meaningful dialogue and action.

That said, this isn't about striving for a win-win, as that is not in anyone's interests. In a kidnap negotiation, I could never agree to a ransom payment for just one of the hostages and forget about the others being held.

How do highly effective people manage their state?

Regardless of whether you are a top executive leading your team of colleagues, a sports coach trying to get the best out of your players in a tournament, or a community worker bringing together a diverse group in support of a worthy cause, all of you have the ability not only to manage your own emotional state, but those of the people around you too. You have an innate ability to see things as they truly are, not worse than they are.

Try asking yourself the following questions as objectively as possible, as if you were reading a news headline:

- What am I dealing with here?

- What is the "story" or "meaning" I'm giving to this? Is it empowering or disempowering?

- How can I see things better than what they currently are, and what does this compelling vision for the future look, sound, and feel like?

- What does my plan of action need to be in order to achieve it?

- Above all else, what kind of person do I need to become in order to make this happen?

The power of emotions

Emotions drive every decision we make, even if we think we're using logic or being completely rational. After all, it's not the physical manifestation of $1 million we seek or the love, the promotion, or the praise for the job well done. It's the emotion we associate with each of those things. We'll be returning to the power emotions have over us and how they can impact our negotiations throughout this book, but for now let's look at what they are.

We are all wired to feel emotions based on our experiences and our interpretation of events (the meaning we give to them). This is why two people can experience exactly the same situation and one person thinks it was the most valuable lesson in their life, whereas the other falls into a spiral of despair. An example of this is experiencing failure. For some, failure can be a shock but they use that energy to work on their weaknesses so they can bounce back stronger. For others, they'll allow negative self-talk to play on a loop inside their minds about how they're not good enough or had no chance of succeeding in the first place.

As we've already mentioned, emotions are simply energy that flood through your body all the time, influencing how you think, feel, and act, both at home and in the workplace. Have you ever lost your temper about something, and, when you reflected on it later, it seemed so trivial? Or perhaps you were feeling low for no apparent reason, or maybe you were disinterested or reluctant about a forthcoming family gathering or business meeting?

Yet many of us lack the ability to accurately recognize and regulate our emotions. The one thing that separates the world's best negotiators and high achievers from those who are less successful is their ability to identify and manage their own emotions, as well as the emotions of those they're negotiating with.

By developing a greater understanding of and relationship with your emotions, you'll be able to harness their power, rather than allowing them to dominate and sabotage you. This will enable you to be more empathetic, creative, and focused on the things and people that matter. Above all, it will enhance your mental well-being and fulfillment. Have I convinced you yet? Are you ready to become curious and learn how to make your emotions your ally, rather than the enemy?

Now would be a good time to take control of your emotions

As the quality of your life is in direct proportion to the quality of your emotions, it makes sense that the more you can understand and have agency over them, the better quality of life you'll experience. It's no exaggeration to say that understanding your emotions and how they influence both your own and others' behavior is a superpower that can enable you to get what you want. Think about that for a moment. Why do you want that promotion? Why do you want to hit your sales target, be in that relationship, earn more money, live in that house, wear that pair of shoes, have that drink, watch that movie?

It's also okay to allow yourself to really feel the emotions. Yet how many of us consciously choose to experience empowering emotions on a consistent basis? Or, as is more often the case, you allow yourself to be triggered and feel disempowering ones instead? Never is this more evident than when you're negotiating with yourself and other people.

There is an abundance of scientific research on human emotions and the reasons you feel what you do in the way you do. Of course, everyone's perception of emotion is slightly different; one person's idea of being in a happy state will be different from another's. Research conducted by Dr. Andrew Huberman of Stanford University found that most theories on emotion come back, in one way or another, to three aspects of the workings of your autonomic nervous system—the part of your nervous system controlling involuntary actions, such as the pumping of your heart. This forms what Huberman calls the "architecture of a feeling." He encourages people to consider the following three questions when they want to understand more accurately what they are feeling and why. There are no right or wrong answers to these questions, as they'll be unique and equally relevant to each and every one of you.

1. How do you feel across a range from high alert to sleepy calm?

2. How "good" or "bad" do you feel?

3. How much of your attention is focused internally on what is going on inside your body, and how much is externally focused in your environment?

An example of internal focus is when you know you are feeling stressed because you are in touch with what's going on inside of your body. You can feel your breathing becoming fast and shallow, for example.

Being externally focused is when, for instance, someone sends you a text message or you read something in the news and you experience a disempowering emotion. Once you've answered the three questions above, you can move on to ask yourself the following two questions:

1. So what?

2. Now what?

These questions are designed to help you develop an acute awareness of how much (and how easily) you allow your environment to impact your emotional state. In reality, the only thing we can truly control is how we respond, based on the meaning we apply to it. The "good" or "bad" elements are simply down to the quality of your stories. Change your story, change your life. And if you don't like your current feeling, then you get to choose a better one.

This is not a case of you waiting until you feel ready before taking action, either. It's about fully embracing the well-proven approach of "mood follows action." Begin the activity or action step irrespective of how you're feeling. By doing so, you will bring about an increase in motivation, and subsequently more empowering emotions, as you progress. For example, you are lying on the couch watching television, yet know you should go for a run or head to the gym. You know this intellectually, but in all honesty, you just can't be bothered. You tell yourself you already went a couple of days ago and you have had a busy day. The exercise can wait, and your favorite show is just about to start, after all. But equally, you could ask yourself how many times you *have* gone for that run or to the gym and felt really good afterward, glad that you made the effort. Mood follows action.

As we now know, small steps consistently applied equals sustained, long-term success as you build on each one. As you see yourself progressing, however small the steps might be, your self-belief and motivation increases. By doing this regularly, you turn it into a habit, which will then keep you going, particularly when you don't feel like it.

Motivation gets you started, but it is habits that keep you going. If you find yourself procrastinating and avoiding preparing for an important meeting or negotiation, don't wait until you feel like doing it. Just start doing something in relation to the task in hand, however small. This may be writing the outline of your opening comments for a presentation or asking your sales department to send you the data you'll be relying on for a forthcoming negotiation. The habits that will help you communicate effectively with anyone, anywhere, on any topic are forged in the daily rituals and routines that reinforce your identity as a negotiator.

Visualize your negotiation success

The brain is like Play-Doh, constantly reshaping. Parts of it can't tell the difference between fully immersive, closed-eye visualization and the real thing. You can see this in the way athletes prepare for a big race. If you watch a downhill skier or a race car driver, for example, they are literally following the course they'll take in their minds, with their bodies physically shifting this way and that with every bend and turn they make in their mind.

On a kidnapping case, I would regularly visualize every aspect of the negotiation from start to finish, particularly the high-risk drop-and-recovery phase, where the ransom money is dropped off at a given location or handed over to one of the kidnappers or their intermediaries before the hostages are released. Such visualization enabled me to plan and prepare as much as I could in order to mitigate the risks as far as possible. Drilling every tiny aspect enabled me and the rest of the CMT to build confidence and certainty in my negotiation strategy.

As you can imagine, there are many moving parts in a drop-and-recovery operation, with plenty of opportunities for things not to go according to plan. In fact, there is very little you can control about what happens. Another added consideration is that such operations are usually conducted without the knowledge of the local police or military, as their involvement often causes more problems and, as previously stated, they are sometimes in cahoots with the kidnappers themselves. Later, you'll learn how best to prepare for negotiations and the types of actions to rehearse until you can do them blindfolded and in your sleep.

There have been many studies into the power of visualization on high performance, particularly in sport. One that often gets cited is from the 1960s at the University of Chicago. Athletes were split into three groups and tested on how many basketball free throws they could make. Afterward, the first group practiced free throws every day for an hour. The second group just visualized themselves making free throws. The third group did nothing. After thirty days, they were tested again. The first group improved by 24 percent. The second group improved by 23 percent without touching a basketball! The third group, as expected, did not improve.

Just as you go to the gym to tone up or lose weight, your ability to have absolute certainty in your vision for success and be in the best possible state is no different from growing muscle. You need to repeat the exercise often because repetition is the mother of all skill. It's the same with any state you want to experience. You must practice it.

By visualizing your success and developing a strong self-belief and certainty, your own potential increases, which in turn means you're more likely to take focused, determined, and impactful action. Once you take that action, guess what results you're going to get? More often than not, you're going to get the results you're looking for or even better. And the cycle continues. When you get these results, what do you think that's going to do for your self-belief and certainty? It's going to increase, and you're going to tell yourself, "See, I knew I *could* do it. I knew it *would* work."

Conversely, if you lack the self-belief, certainty, and confidence, and you can't visualize success ahead of time, you also lack belief in your own potential, take minimal action, and, therefore, get poor results. Then what happens? You end up telling yourself, "See, I knew I *couldn't* do it. I knew it *wouldn't* work."

Managing your state in a kidnapping

In a kidnap-for-ransom negotiation, I knew that I had to have unswerving levels of self-belief and certainty about my ability to advise the client and negotiate the release of the hostages. This wasn't the same as being arrogant or not being open to new ideas. Nor was it about being inflexible in my suggested plan. It was about having the resilient mindset that no matter what happened, I would always find a way to make it work, to ensure that I advised and recommended the best course of action that I could. In fact, in every case, I made sure the client was actively involved in forming the best possible negotiation strategy based on the circumstances and context.

Whenever I arrived in-country to advise the client, there would always be a palpable sigh of relief as I walked in the door, as if the cavalry was here and that everything would be okay. Imagine if I walked into the room full of self-doubt and portraying an air of nervousness and indecision. How do you think being in that state would have impacted the quality of my actions and those of the client?

Whenever the kidnappers threatened to execute one of the hostages by the end of the day, I needed a high degree of positivity and state management. When do you think I began using a resilient mindset to get into such a state? On the plane? In the taxi from the airport? Just before I walked in and met the family and CMT? No. I did it even before I received the initial phone call to be deployed.

Every day, I still make sure I train my mind to focus on more empowering rather than disempowering thoughts and beliefs. It really does just come down to a question of intent and setting high standards; not perfection, though, as that is, in fact, the lowest standard of all and doesn't exist. It was deciding that I was, more often than not, going to stay in control of my mind and respond accordingly, no matter what happened. This hadn't always been the case, though. Far from it, in fact.

* * *

Negotiation Case File #2: United Kingdom

The sun wasn't yet up, but within minutes of receiving the phone call, I was speeding my way to an apartment in east London, a three-bedroom flat housing a family of nine. One of the teenage sons had got into trouble with a notorious drug gang that ruled the area and been abducted off the street a few hours earlier. Not long afterward, his brother, Jackson, began receiving phone calls from an unknown number demanding £50,000. It was my first kidnapping case and my first time inside a Red Center.

I arrived to chaos; loads of people were crammed into the flat. The mother was sobbing, and it was obvious that Jackson knew more than he was letting on. Not long after I got there, the kidnappers sent through a short film clip of his brother having a hot iron pressed firmly against his chest. The piercing screams rang around the tiny flat. The family bundled the now-hysterical mother into the hallway so she wouldn't have to see or hear any more of her son being tortured. All eyes were on me and a more experienced officer and negotiator, Steve, the Red Center Commander, to make their pain go away. Easier said than done.

My heart felt like it was beating so loudly that the neighbors would complain about the noise. I also felt a churning in my stomach and my body was tense and rigid with nerves. As the day wore on, the family refused to follow our advice and I started to get frustrated. I reminded them, in what could only be described as a forceful tone, of how important it was for them to trust us if they wanted their beloved son and brother back safely. Steve gently placed his hand on my shoulder and gave it an almost imperceptible squeeze. It was enough to interrupt my pattern and alleviate the lousy state I'd allowed myself to get into. In that moment, I understood that I couldn't help the family if I didn't stay calm and in control of my emotions.

Without truly realizing it at the time, I was experiencing a steady buildup of stress and anxiety stemming from a perceived lack of control. Left unchecked, mine would've been the shortest career ever in kidnap negotiation. Steve, however, who had years of experience in successfully negotiating such situations, exuded a quiet, yet confident air. While I may have initially struggled to keep my own emotions in check, I realized that I needed to watch, study, and learn from him, and fast.

He sat Jackson down and began writing something on a piece of paper with a thick marker pen.

"This is the only thing I want you to focus on. The rest will follow, okay?" Steve said, holding the paper up to him.

Jackson smiled and relaxed. I leaned forward to take a look. There, written in big black letters, was one word.

BREATHE.

Steve then slowly took him through our three objectives for the next call with the kidnappers, apart from breathing properly, that is.

First, reassure the kidnappers that we, too, wanted to resolve the situation. Doing this would put the bad guys at ease and in a more positive state.

Second, we needed proof that they did, in fact, have the hostage and that he was alive. This was crucial, because otherwise you end up paying for a corpse or to people who aren't physically holding the hostage and who are, therefore, unable to release him.

Third, we wanted to establish a call window in which we would speak to the kidnappers again. Otherwise, the nerves of everyone in the Red Center would be shot to bits waiting for hours or days for the phone to ring.

Usually, we like to keep the rest of the family out of the way at this stage so that their emotions don't rub off on the negotiator. However, by effectively harnessing what I would later discover was his own inner Red Center, Steve brought about a level of calm, not only in himself, but also among the family. He demonstrated an awareness and willingness to take responsibility for what needed to be done, an ability to stay focused on the desired outcome, and, above all else, to dig deep and bring to bear sufficient levels of mental and emotional resilience in a life-or-death situation.

His actions and demeanor reassured everyone present and showed the family (and me) that resilience in times of challenge and high stress begins in the mind. To step into the eye of the storm and bring calm to your world, even if everyone around you is losing it, is to make and implement effective decisions.

By now the family had also come around to his way of thinking. By including them in the strategies and decision-making process, they felt they were being listened to, that their voices were being heard, and that they and their loved ones mattered. This inner calm continued to be tested, though. On one call, it became clear that the kidnappers knew our exact location and that the police were helping the family to negotiate the release. For this, they threatened to send some gang members around to "spray the place with a Mac-10," the weapon of choice at the time for a number of London gangs. This is a deadly weapon that can fire 1,400 bullets a minute. Only one needs to hit its target for it to be game over.

Despite this, the family didn't want to relocate, even after we offered them a safe five-star hotel overlooking the Thames River at no cost to themselves. I realized that even in the face of an extreme threat, they wanted to be in the comfort of their own space. Again, in the eye of this new storm, a clear head was needed. While the threat issued against us may have been only that, I didn't want to take any chances. We threw discretion out the window and arranged for two BMW X5 armed response vehicles to be parked directly outside the entrance to the flat.

In these vehicles sat six heavily armed police officers carrying more fire-power than a small army. As they sat there, engines purring and weapons at the ready, it allowed me to settle into the right frame of mind and focus my energies on working with Steve to plan the delicate negotiations neces-sary to get the brother released as quickly as possible.

In the United Kingdom, kidnappings rarely last longer than a week. This case, however, was still going strong at the five-day point, with no end in sight. In the Red Center, Steve and I were deliberately kept in the dark by HQ about the other intelligence being worked up or the tactics being planned, including the possibility of a hostage rescue. This was to avoid us unintentionally revealing anything to either the family or the kidnappers through a subtle shift in our tone of voice, behavior, or energy.

As mentioned earlier, most first-world police forces and military units have excellent, highly trained teams capable of carrying out such high-risk operations—not always without casualties, though. The chances of success in some of the more challenging parts of the world were, however, much lower. As this case was in London, the Metropolitan Police's specialist fire-arms officers from the elite CO19 unit (as it was known at the time) were standing by and ready for action.

The phone rang and, while Jackson answered it, I pressed "Record" on the small device attached to the phone. Not only is making a record-ing great evidence in any future prosecution, it's also useful to play back and listen to again to clarify something if there is a dispute or uncer-tainty about what has been said. It also enabled us to listen for any back-ground noise that could enable us to identify where the kidnappers were calling from or even holding the hostage, although this is often a sepa-rate location.

Steve sat on Jackson's right with his left knee almost touching his. This wasn't because he wanted an inappropriately timed game of footsie, but rather a tried-and-tested way of keeping the negotiator grounded.

"You ready to pay?" said a male voice on the other end of the phone.

"Almost. We'll be ready soon," said Jackson.

"When?"

"Probably tomorrow."

Steve almost fell off his chair. Jackson was going off-script. While the communicator acting on behalf of the family or company is encouraged to ad-lib as required on these calls, what they can't do is start making decisions. Indicating a possible timeline, without this previously being agreed to or, more importantly, planned for by the CMT, only increases the chances of us not being able to meet it. This will in turn antagonize the kidnappers even more and erode any hard-won trust we might have managed to establish with them.

While we'd managed to get the kidnapper's demands down to £30,000, the family had only managed to collect half of that.

Steve nudged his knee against Jackson's and scribbled a note.

DELAY IT.

Credit to Jackson, he thought on his feet.

"Tomorrow's Sunday, so the banks will be shut; more likely Monday or Tuesday."

"Location of drop on Monday. Don't f . . . us about."

The notes kept coming and the knee stayed firmly in place.

BREATHE.

ASK TO SPEAK TO YOUR BROTHER.

"Put him on, yeah. I need proof," Jackson asked the kidnapper.

"You've had proof. You get it when you pay the money."

There was no way any money would be paid until the brother had been spoken to. Steve shook his head and encouraged Jackson to keep talking.

"No proof, no money."

Silence. We had to keep our nerve. Otherwise, the kidnappers would smell fear and abuse it.

The call ended abruptly.

Before we could offer any explanation, the phone screen lit up again.

Jackson answered.

"Hello?" said a different voice, barely above a whisper.

"Hey, you doing good? You got this. You're going to be okay," said Jackson, visibly relieved to hear his brother's voice.

"They done me up bad," said his brother.

"Enough," interrupted an aggressive voice. "Monday or you'll never see him again."

With that, the call was ended.

Jackson looked to Steve and then to me, as if pleading for reassurance or a sign that everything would be okay. Steve and I exchanged glances, both of us knowing that we were about to enter the endgame.

Two hours later, it was all over. The location of the stronghold where the brother was being tortured had been identified and that final call was enough for senior officers back at Scotland Yard to be concerned that his life was in imminent danger. Furthermore, the money still wasn't ready. CO19 had been given the green light. This meant that there would now be only one outcome.

Having dropped Jackson at the hospital to see his brother after he'd been examined by the doctors, Steve and I made our excuses and left. After the high-fives, hugs, and handshakes, there was no point hanging around like a stale smell. Family and colleagues just want to return to normal as quickly as possible, and we were just a reminder of a bad dream. All cases, no matter how high-pressure they felt at the time, always strengthened my resilience muscles even further, knowing that it wouldn't be long before the next challenge would show up, requiring me to utilize them all over again.

* * *

Whatever you focus on creates your reality

In all negotiations, I would continuously encourage the client to focus not only on the things they can control, but also on the language they use within the CMT and Red Center, rather than spiraling into negative despair, however understandable that may have been. Even in times of crisis, conflict, or significant change, you still get to control the meaning you give things and your subsequent response. One way you can enhance this is by the quality of the language you use, particularly the questions you ask yourself when faced with a challenging situation:

- Is this a problem or an opportunity?

- Is this the end or the beginning?

- What's the gift or learning from this?

- Am I focusing on what I have or what's missing?

- What can or can't I control right now?

Taking such an approach is probably best exemplified by Viktor Frankl, the Austrian psychotherapist, Holocaust survivor, and author of *Man's Search for Meaning*, who said: "Between stimulus and response there is a space. In that space is our power to choose our response. In our response lies our growth and our freedom."

Despite witnessing and personally experiencing horrific torture in a concentration camp, he observed his fellow inmates extensively both during captivity and upon release. He found that those who not only survived but then went on to live a happy and normal life afterward were able to master this "space" because it enabled them to harness and develop a more positive meaning from their circumstances, however horrific they may have appeared on the surface. These people had discovered their *why* for living.

If you don't have an empowering future, you lose all hope. People feel depressed because they can't visualize having such a future, nor do they have a big enough "why" pulling them through tough times and out the other side. Frankl believed that the secret was to find a better meaning in something outside and bigger than yourself, whether that something is a loved one, close friend, teammate, long-standing and loyal client, or a worthy cause close to you.

See if you can apply this principle next time you enter a negotiation. Ask yourself honestly, are you really focusing on the benefits to the other person or simply thinking about how much commission you'll make from the deal? We'll go into further detail later in the book about how you can develop this "space" within a negotiation or any form of communication to allow yourself to *respond* most appropriately, rather than merely *react* in a habitual and often unhelpful way.

How your emotions impact your negotiations

It's worth spending some time now exploring why you communicate the way that you do, so you can then learn to take control and negotiate far more effectively. Up until recently, it was an accepted idea that our emotions are hardwired into us through evolution, ready to be activated following specific triggers. However, a growing body of evidence is now revealing how we construct emotions based on our own individual "models of the world." These we construct through a combination of our values, beliefs, rules, life experiences, and so on.

For example, two individuals will experience the same situation in completely different ways and experience different emotions with different effects on their bodies. Therefore the actions they subsequently take will likely be different based on whatever meaning they've assigned to that particular situation.

Language

The language you use, not just in a negotiation but in everyday life, will absolutely dictate the quality and often the outcome of that event. Ultimately, you're a meaning-making machine and the way you create or assign meaning is through your use of language. Because, if you haven't realized it yet, words matter. They matter so much, in fact, that people are prepared to live and die by them. Consider your own choice of words to describe certain emotions and the impact they have on you.

Do you find yourself frequently using terms such as "good" or "bad" or "right" or "wrong" or "always," "never," "should"? If so, it's time to expand your emotional vocabulary. This is you taking back control and choosing a far more inspiring way to talk about your experiences and in your negotiations, simply by changing the words you use to interpret or describe them. Like any skill, it takes practice—if you want to build muscle, you need to go to the gym. Not just once, but consistently. Building your emotional vocabulary is no different.

Negative Belief-Buster Exercise

If you catch yourself stuck in an emotional story that you can't seem to get out of, such as when you're blaming or criticizing someone else for how you feel, consider asking the following three questions that will help you create a little distance and reframe the story. You'll take back control of your emotions and how you subsequently communicate.

1. What are the *facts* about what happened? Consider what really happened, without any analysis or interpretation. Think of this as if it were an innocuous news headline, such as, "Man takes four hours to reply to his wife's text message."

2. What is the *meaning* you gave to the facts? This allows you to explore and clarify your model of the world, the beliefs and rules you have about what should and shouldn't happen. For example, "If he loved me, he'd have replied to my message sooner. He must be messaging someone else. I'm clearly not a priority in his life."

3. What was your *reaction* to the meaning you gave to the facts? "I felt angry and jealous, and when he did message me, instead of being concerned for his welfare and checking that he was okay first, I immediately reacted by sending him lots of abusive and unreasonable messages. This led to an argument and only resulted in reinforcing my story. In reality, there was a poor phone signal and no Wi-Fi where he was traveling. His battery had run out, too, and I know that his phone is old and it doesn't hold its charge that well."

(Continued)

The focus needs to be on mastering your beliefs (meaning), which in turn determine your response, rather than the stimulus, which in this example is the length of time taken to receive a reply. This is because nothing has any meaning except the meaning you choose to give it, so you have to take ownership of the meaning you give things. There are no excuses with this, only choices or stories, because the emotion you feel, whether suffering or joy, will come from the meaning you give the situation and not the situation itself.

Belief-busting assignment

Get to the root of your patterns by recording at least one stimulus response pattern each day for a week. Notice that when you swap or reframe your old disempowering beliefs for an empowering one, you have the power to create a story that adds value, rather than causing you frustration or some other disempowering emotion. Remember, you get to shape your stories, so choose wisely.

For example, "I've *got* to do all this preparation for an important meeting tomorrow with a potential client, but I don't have enough time and am starting to feel overwhelmed." You can reframe this into "I *get* to develop a deeper understanding of how I can best serve this client, which, if they sign the contract, means our business will be able to grow, develop, and bring our wonderful product to even more people." Remember, the power is in the reframe.

Technique 3: Developing Emotional Intelligence to Improve Your Negotiation Skills

Developing your emotional intelligence (EQ) is crucial if you want to become the best negotiator you can be *and* a master communicator. If this isn't enough of a motivator for you, EQ is also considered a great predictor of success in life, even more so than a person's intellectual intelligence (IQ).

A relatively recent term, EQ was first established in 1990, when the Yale psychologists Peter Salovey and John Mayer articulated a theory of emotional intelligence and defined it as the "ability to identify feelings and emotions in oneself and others, and to use this information to guide your behavior." Another perspective of EQ is summed up nicely by the mindfulness expert Jon Kabat-Zinn, who describes it as "the development of empathy and the de-coding of emotions and underlying motivations in oneself and others."

What is emotional intelligence, and why is it important for effective negotiation?

Emotional intelligence consists of four domains:

1. Self-awareness and internal motivation

2. Self-management and regulation

3. Empathy and relationship management

4. Social skills and awareness

Determining somebody's EQ score is not like completing an IQ test. In an IQ test, you either get the numerical or verbal reasoning questions correct or you don't. Establishing EQ is more complex; nevertheless, I'm sure you can all think of somebody who:

- Remains calm in highly stressful or emotional situations.

- Takes ownership for how they feel and therefore how they respond in any given moment, rather than blaming others for making them feel a certain way.

- Once you've finished a conversation or meeting with them, you feel like you've been seen, heard, and understood—that they "get" you.

These are just some of the behaviors an emotionally intelligent person might display. They can be significant factors in a person's success in both the home and workplace. So, what enables them to exhibit this behavior?

FIGURE 1-1

The four domains of emotional intelligence

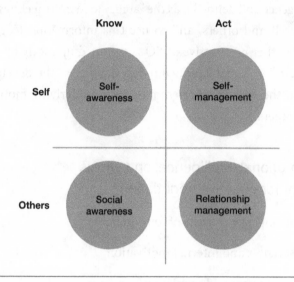

They have simply mastered the four EQ domains, which are illustrated in figure 1-1. Developing and consistently practicing these same four skill areas will make you a more emotionally intelligent person and thereby a more effective negotiator.

Most, if not all, of the kidnap negotiations I was involved in featured confrontation, threats, and verbal abuse directed toward me and my colleagues. Allowing these to wash over us and not take hold was paramount. Again, this was about parking the ego and truly listening to what the other side was saying, as well as identifying the underlying needs they were asking us to meet.

This is no different from a business negotiation. If both sides are stuck on a particular issue or if one party feels like the other is taking advantage of them, tensions will run high. Threats can manifest themselves in many different ways in a negotiation. One party might walk away from the deal or present a take-it-or-leave-it offer. Both are usually driven by fear, which stems from a lack of self-regulation and empathy.

This approach also applies in the home when you're negotiating with your kids about going to bed or reducing screen time on their devices. Most human behavior is driven by the fear of loss (followed to a lesser degree by the motivation to experience pleasure). We fear that somehow we are going to miss out on something or it might be taken away from us or that we'll have less of it.

Regardless of whether we are negotiating with kidnappers, colleagues, potential clients, or our kids, if we can identify what it is they fear to lose the most from the "deal," then we can begin to start influencing their behavior. This, of course, applies to yourself, too. Which is why it's important to ask yourself the same question, because once you know what you fear to lose the most in any given situation—perhaps it's freedom, reputation, money—you will be able to manage the emotions that might show up and get in the way of negotiating a successful deal, such as frustration, jealousy, or anger, for example.

Imagine EQ as being divided into two categories: the *self* and *others*, with *self* including internal motivation, self-awareness, and self-regulation and *others* covering social awareness and relationship management.

Self: Internal motivation, self-awareness, and self-motivation

Internal motivation

Internal motivation is being able to make yourself work with minimal pressure from others. This might include harnessing your curiosity, an overwhelming desire to fulfill your potential, or wanting to see your creation come to life. While you may want to be rewarded for your efforts with money or praise, they aren't the driving force behind your behavior. This means you have more control over your productivity, because your motivation is self-generated.

Self-awareness

Self-awareness is the ability to evaluate yourself and understand how your behavior is being perceived by others. If you're self-aware, you know how you're feeling, how you're acting, and how you appear to others. You likely have a strong grasp of your own strengths and weaknesses, which means that you know where and how you'll be most useful to others. This knowledge can make you a great leader, because you have an understanding of what skills you may be missing and therefore where and how you need others to apply their skills.

Self-awareness can also help you train yourself to think about your emotions in a productive way. It requires self-reflection and interpretation, so if you're self-aware, when you get upset, you might start to think about why you feel as you do. This gives you the opportunity to discover that the feeling is momentary, misplaced, or useful as a catalyst for positive action. Doing this allows you to think of your emotions as part of a larger picture, so you don't become consumed by them. Knowing the reasoning behind your emotions can also give you a greater sense of control over them, improving self-efficacy.

Develop your emotional self-awareness

The ancient Greek philosopher Socrates asserted that one of the most important aspects of human existence is to "know thyself." Such a statement goes to the very heart of what EQ, and therefore effective negotiation, are all about. In fact, it could be argued that it's the foundation of it. Imagine how much calmer and uplifting the home or workplace would be if people had greater levels of self-awareness, particularly when negotiating with one another.

On a tense and highly emotive kidnapping case, if I walked into the room where the CMT or family were set up and didn't have that finely tuned sensory acuity and self-awareness, I would've lost credibility and their trust (and struggled to regain it), which was crucial to the success of the negotiation.

Developing such an awareness is made more difficult by your inability to remain focused on one thing for any length of time. When that report you are drafting has an impending deadline, have you ever found yourself first checking your emails, before getting that irresistible urge to scroll through social media and then opening a WhatsApp message from one of the many group chats you're in? Then, when you attempt to get back to that report—hang on, it's nearly lunchtime and you're hungry. And so it goes on.

Like any habit worth forging, self-awareness takes discipline. It requires you to raise your standards and be clear that you'll no longer tolerate certain excuses. We're not talking about perfectionism here; far from it, as perfectionism is the *lowest* standard, as it is driven by fear wrapped in a lack of self-worth.

- What scenarios can you think of where, if you'd had higher levels of self-awareness, you would have fared better? What did that emotional outburst or comment cost you?

- How committed are you on a scale of 1 (low) to 10 (high) to increase your self-awareness, which will ultimately help you be in control of your emotions, rather than allowing them to hijack and control you?

Self-regulation

Self-regulation (also known as emotional balance) is the ability to remain calm in emotionally trying situations. This ability to keep your disruptive emotions and impulses in check and maintain your effectiveness under stressful or even hostile conditions is an unbelievable superpower. With emotional balance, you recognize the disruptive emotions that get in your way—like high anxiety, intense fear, or anger—and you find ways to manage your emotions and impulses.

While many factors influence how you feel and may be beyond your control, if you're highly self-regulated, you're good at controlling your reactions. You can make clearheaded decisions, even if things are falling apart around you. Also, if you're highly self-regulated, you can easily adapt, because the discomfort that often comes from change won't make you stumble. Self-regulation is a necessary skill for people whose jobs are fast-paced and dangerous. For example, you would want to be self-regulated as a firefighter. If, when faced with a fire, you panic, you could hyperventilate and pass out, endangering yourself and those you are trying to save.

How to increase emotional self-regulation

The first step in developing self-regulation is by creating stillness, in both your body and mind. Simple, but not easy, right? When you allow yourself to be taken an emotional hostage, like in the lack of focus example above, waves of cortisol and dopamine, among other powerful chemicals, are pumped around your body. These can affect you in different ways, depending on when you experience them and in what doses.

Dopamine, often referred to as the happy drug, regulates mood and muscle movement, playing a vital role in the brain's pleasure and reward systems. Used effectively, it can encourage you to take action and follow through, yet it can also lead to addiction, and therefore unhelpful and inappropriate thoughts, feelings, and behaviors. The more you experience the rush that the drug provides, the more you'll crave it, and so the vicious circle continues. Every time you cross something off your to-do list or receive a "like" for a post on social media, your brain rewards you with a wave of dopamine.

When you factor this into a high-pressure situation or challenging conversation, your brain is likely to hijack your cognitive ability and will stumble into survival mode, becoming addicted to taking action (any action) and seeking instant gratification, often because you want to feel or be seen to be significant, not because that particular activity is important. Remember, dopamine doesn't distinguish between activity and productivity. As a seminal *Harvard Business Review* article "Beware the Busy Manager" reveals, most leaders think they're being effective and prioritizing, "but in reality, they're just spinning their wheels."

As Rasmus Hougaard, the founder and CEO of one of the world's top leadership development consultancies, Potential Project, says, "Action addiction is one of the biggest threats to our mental effectiveness." He goes on to explain that one of the antidotes is for us to consciously choose what we want to focus on and then focus on what we've chosen. When distractions then arise, so be it. We get to consciously choose whether we allow our focus to dwell there or not.

Cortisol, also called the stress drug, is produced in your adrenal gland, located just above the kidneys. It helps you maintain a healthy blood pressure and immune function, strengthens your heart muscle, and supports your body's anti-inflammatory processes. You also get extra doses of cortisol when faced with those fight, flight, or freeze moments. This is designed to *increase* your blood pressure, heart rate, and muscle tension and shut down your digestive system, so your body can literally survive and overcome whatever challenge or "threat" you may be facing.

Levels then return to normal after you've swerved to miss the oncoming car, met the deadline, or pressed "Send" on that all-important report to your boss. High levels of cortisol are not necessarily a bad thing. When you wake up first thing in the morning, your body naturally produces cortisol, which is essential for regulating your levels of energy, focus, and immune system function. It is usually at its highest level at this point and gradually decreases throughout the day. It is also released during exercise and, in small doses, it can also heighten memory and lower sensitivity to pain.

Dr. Steve Peters, author of *The Chimp Paradox*, explains, "[Stress] is actually a healthy reaction that is meant to be uncomfortable. It is nature's way of telling you something is wrong and that you need to act to put it right. You may find this manifests itself as aggression, impatience, anxiety or low mood." Producing cortisol is just one of the body's natural ways of responding to such stress.

The challenge arises when you allow your cortisol level to remain high for lengthy periods of time, particularly into the late afternoon and evening, without releasing some of that tension or stress. If left unchecked, persistently high cortisol levels can lead to many negative side effects, including elevated blood sugar levels (hyperglycemia), for example, which in turn can cause type 2 diabetes.

If you can master emotional self-regulation, you can offset the negative effects of dopamine and cortisol and be more resilient in the face of adversity. One way of doing this is by increasing another naturally produced and equally powerful neurotransmitter called serotonin, which helps regulate your mood, body temperature, and appetite.

Serotonin is our body's way of balancing out the negative effects of dopamine and cortisol, as it provides high levels of clarity and inhibits impulsive behaviors. It also reduces feelings of depression and anxiety. How can you increase your levels of serotonin? By regularly training the mind and body to resist the impulses to indulge in distracting thoughts and by letting go of unproductive stress. In doing so, serotonin will be produced in your brain and balance out the dopamine and cortisol spikes.

Ultimately, this is about learning to respond consciously and with full awareness, rather than a knee-jerk, habitual reaction. This is not about living like a monk! Quite the opposite, as it means you can respond to situations, people, and events you don't like without becoming stressed and emotional. Maintaining serotonin levels enables you to remain calm, balanced, and grounded at the center of any storm, leaving you feeling more focused, emotionally stable, and happier.

This stillness can be cultivated by taking as little as thirty seconds to pause and check in with yourself before you walk into an important negotiation or client meeting, or in the space between when you've finished one task and before you move onto the next.

1. Pause.

2. Take a couple of deep breaths, fully exhaling with each one.

3. Allow your shoulders to drop and relax.

4. Notice whatever feeling is showing up in your body.

Is there a slight churning in your stomach or a dull ache in your neck, or perhaps you feel yourself becoming tense and irritable? If so, feel the feeling and drop whichever story you're associating it with.

I did this exercise every time, just before I walked into the CMT room where I would wait for the kidnappers to call. And when the phone did ring, I would get the communicator answering it to do a shorter version of this for a couple of seconds, just so he could regulate his nervous system and control his emotions.

Another option that often works is to set random reminders on your phone to nudge you into stopping whatever you happen to be doing so that you can check in with curious awareness with whatever you're feeling in your body. Once you do so, you must acknowledge and take full responsibility for your feeling, as it has absolutely nothing to do with any other person, however harmful or wrong you may think they are.

Remember, the impact the emotion has on you is determined by the meaning you give it. This is different from acquiescing or agreeing with someone. Rather, it is a case of acknowledging and taking ownership of the one thing you have absolute control over: how you respond in any given moment.

Others: Empathy and relationship management

Empathy

Empathy is often misunderstood as sympathy, but it's not the same thing. To empathize is to attempt to genuinely understand how others are feeling, often by picking up both verbal and nonverbal cues in their language and behavior, including sensing unspoken emotions.

People with high levels of empathy will usually get along well with people of very different backgrounds and cultures and can express their ideas in ways other people will understand. While no one can know for sure if they're feeling what someone else is, if you're highly empathetic, you're also good at intuiting what their feelings might be and how they see things.

Is empathy a bad thing?

Not everyone considers empathy to be a helpful means of communicating and developing rapport. Some even argue that it can be selective, biased, or even dangerous as well as being highly subjective, leading to poor decision-making because we don't all understand and feel what others are going through to the same degree.

In my experience, however, this completely misses the point of what empathy is about. To empathize with someone, I don't have to feel anything toward them, as it's more about perceiving and understanding their emotions and not necessarily experiencing the same for myself. This is more akin to sympathy, where, for example, I might feel sorry for a friend who is going through a rough time in their marriage.

Empathy has also been described as the doorway to compassion, through which you need to walk in order to understand emotions in the same way as the person experiencing them. Through this doorway lies the ability to feel what that person is feeling, to hold and accept it as if it were your own. Essentially, you might consider compassion as being empathy in action.

In a high-stakes negotiation, however, if I start to feel sympathy or compassion toward the hostages and their families, or even the kidnappers themselves, this is likely to cloud my thinking and prevent me from doing my job effectively. This is why empathy is so powerful, because it allows me to still see things from another person's perspective, yet at the same time remain objective, rational, and focused on the bigger picture, rather than allowing myself to go on a rollercoaster of emotions. This is no different in any negotiation you may find yourself in.

In order to be empathetic, I have to demonstrate and articulate to the other person what I believe their experience is, not in some Machiavellian or mischievous way, but with the right intention of truly understanding what, how, and why they think, feel, and behave the way they do, even if I disagree with them. From this place, I can communicate with them far more effectively and enable them to feel safe, seen, heard, and understood, right here, right now in the present moment. Only then are we ready to negotiate.

An easy way to differentiate between compassion, sympathy, and empathy is to see sympathy and its close cousin compassion as being feelings (from the heart) you share with another person: "I'm so sorry for your loss. That's an awful thing to have happened." Whereas empathy is being able to demonstrate an understanding of the emotions being experienced by another person (from your head): "It sounds like you are really upset with what happened."

Empathy is simply the identification of another's situation, motive, and emotion and then demonstrating your understanding of this back to them. It doesn't matter if you get it wrong, as it's more about your *attempt* to get it right that is important. This in turn creates a positive atmosphere for problem-solving. We'll cover some specific techniques that can assist you further in achieving this later in the book.

How to develop empathy

Empathy is a doing word. It's something that you do in order to tune in to another person's world, like searching for a radio signal you don't know the frequency for. It's how you manage yourself and your relationship with others, which is key to sustained high performance and outstanding leadership and negotiation.

An example of how you can apply this learning to everyday situations is perhaps when you are faced with an irate client. Maybe they haven't received the level of service or outcome they were expecting, and now they're expressing their displeasure. While you may feel that they're overreacting and that it wasn't your fault, remember that people can't listen when they're in a highly emotional state, such as anger or frustration. The key is to remain calm by managing your own state and avoiding an ego-driven verbal slanging match with them. Once you've controlled your own state, it's time to demonstrate empathy toward them. To reiterate, it doesn't matter if you don't agree with or even like them.

Opportunities for demonstrating empathetic behavior, including having conversations driven by a desire to first understand before being understood, present themselves multiple times every single day. Yet often the default culture within many workplaces today involves people competing with one another, protecting their silos, budgets, or resources rather than focusing on deep collaboration with others toward achieving a common goal or outcome; namely, adding more value to their clients and customers than anyone else does, thereby creating an extreme competitive advantage and dominating their particular industry.

This is usually driven by leaders lacking the courage to have difficult conversations with their staff and, crucially, with themselves. Also, by developing a depth and consistency of courage to accept that they don't need to have all the answers, leaders can demonstrate psychological safety, which, as Daniel Coyle argues in *The Culture Code*, is an essential ingredient in producing highly successful groups.

This can be achieved by enabling and facilitating others through open and honest dialogue, rather than relying on the often subconscious drive to exhibit coercive power and control. It isn't rocket science. Who can honestly say that they wouldn't prefer to be spoken to in a calm, friendly, empathetic way by someone who sees us for who we are, as an individual, and encourages us to do our best work? Why, then, is it so simple, yet not so easy to apply all the time? Because we ignore and fail to address the primary emotions present in any given communication.

As we've already highlighted, you can't truly influence and persuade somebody until you first manage your own and then their emotions. The *negotiation balance* image shown in figure 1-2 how you can begin to do so. This is particularly useful when either you or the other person you are attempting to negotiate with is overwhelmed and in a state of heightened anxiety, frustration, anger, or stress. Consider that all communication can be distilled down to either being:

- A *"cry for help,"* such as having negative thoughts or feelings that are demonstrated through words or actions, including shouting, arguing, frustration, stonewalling, or being passive-aggressive. Usually, the person will not realize that they are even making such a cry for help, as it's a habitual pattern hardwired into them over many years.

- Or a *"loving response,"* such as demonstrating active listening, where your focus is on nothing except truly hearing and empathizing with what the other person is saying and, crucially, what is not being said. This in turn enables them to feel seen, heard, and understood.

Until you can address their cry for help in this way, calm, rational, objective thought is impossible. They simply cannot hear the words being spoken.

As the image shows, you first need to reduce the anxiety and stress of the other person before any calm, objective, rational thinking or behavior will ever take place. It's only when objective rational thought increases that you can begin to start influencing and bringing about some form of behavioral change in that person. The same approach is equally effective in business negotiations and dealing with your teenage kids as it is with hostile kidnappers.

The emotional and rational parts of the brain are linked via strong neural pathways. One is not necessarily more important than the other, as your ability to develop your emotional intelligence is dependent on these pathways. When the emotions begin to get out of hand, the rational side will interject and correct them. This is why emotionally balanced people with a high degree of emotional intelligence can usually stop themselves from saying something they'll later regret, despite having the emotive urge to do so.

FIGURE 1-2

Negotiation balance

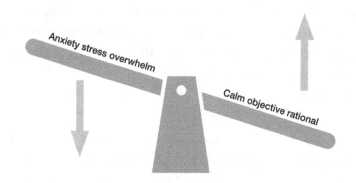

Others: *Social awareness*

Social awareness is the ability to pick up on social cues and negotiate well with others. It requires being quick on one's feet in conversations. Socially aware people are often very good listeners who can easily figure out what's important to the people they speak with. If you're socially aware, you're also good at perceiving formal and informal power structures, group dynamics, and appealing to the right people. As such, social awareness is a powerful tool that can lead you to fit in, thrive, and potentially become a powerful leader and negotiator.

- Emotions make intelligent people say and do stupid things.

- When people are perceived as being irrational, but reacting to the world as they see it, they are simply experiencing powerful emotions.

- When people are emotional, they can't always listen properly.

- When they can't listen, they can't be persuaded.

- So your words are useless, until you have demonstrated empathy and dealt with their emotions.

Chapter Summary

By consistently developing your resilience, emotional self-regulation, and a centered state of equanimity, you will cultivate a winning mindset capable of navigating crises, conflicts, and uncertainties with ease. Above all, you will become a master negotiator.

To achieve this:

DEVELOP YOUR RESILIENCE: Develop a sense of balance and calm within yourself by harnessing your inner Red Center. If you do, you'll maintain focus, quickly adapt to changing situations, and respond effectively.

- **Acknowledge** and **accept** any physical sensations of tension or discomfort in your body.

- **Breathe** through these sensations.

- **Clarify** the triggers, enabling you to cultivate calmness, intuition, and presence, tapping into your inner resourcefulness to achieve negotiation success.

CHOOSE YOUR FOCUS: Whatever you focus on and give meaning to will shape your reality. Therefore, choose wisely where to direct your attention and the interpretation you give to events and situations. By shifting your perspective and viewing challenges as opportunities, problems as potential solutions, and crises as chances for growth, you can develop and maintain a positive and empowering mindset, even in the face of adversity.

When faced with challenges and obstacles, ask better questions and you'll get better answers:

- What am I not seeing here?

- What else could this mean?

- Where is the opportunity in this?

- What is the learning?

ENHANCE YOUR EMOTIONAL SELF-REGULATION: This is the number one skill required of all highly effective negotiators. Emotional intelligence plays a vital role in negotiation success. Being aware of your own emotions and those of others allows for more effective communication and understanding. You'll maintain your composure, demonstrate empathy, build rapport easily, and ultimately make more rational decisions, creating an environment conducive to productive negotiations.

- Action Steps: Take the time for self-reflection and practice mindfulness, which is crucial for developing emotional self-regulation.

You will then be able to respond consciously rather than react impulsively. To achieve this:

- Create stillness in your body and mind.

- Allow distracting thoughts to come and go without judgment.

- Pause before important negotiations or meetings to check in with yourself, acknowledging and taking responsibility for whatever feelings arise. Also do this when you've finished a task and before moving onto the next.

- Set random reminders on your phone to nudge you.

- Park your ego. Set aside personal agendas and demonstrate empathy toward others. This creates an atmosphere of trust and collaboration, leading to more favorable negotiation outcomes.

Key Takeaways

1. Harness your inner Red Center to develop a sense of balance and calm despite the storm raging around you.

2. Whatever you focus on and give meaning to will create your reality. So choose wisely.

3. Emotional self-regulation is the primary skill of all highly effective negotiators.

CHAPTER TWO

Preparing to Win Every Negotiation

There is a well-known saying that, in a crisis, most of us don't rise to the occasion, but rather fall to our highest level of preparation. It is also well understood that no matter what you do to prepare, other people will often fail to do what you expect them to, and therefore things are likely to not go according to plan. This usually takes people by surprise in a negotiation, because they're approaching it with a fixed mindset, rather than one of curiosity, agility, and a desire to truly understand the other person's "model of the world"—how and what they see, interpret, and give meaning to.

While having this approach is fundamental to succeeding in any negotiation, it won't be enough by itself. To consistently succeed at the very highest level also requires you and your team to learn, develop, and practice the required knowledge, skills, and techniques. It's no use waiting until the crunch moment and then looking around wondering what you should do next.

In this chapter, you'll do a deep dive into three key techniques that will increase your chances of negotiation success by preparing yourself and your teams not only to withstand some of the challenges that occur in any form of negotiation, but to thrive and approach them with a mindset of constant and never-ending improvement or, as the old military adage goes, the unrelenting pursuit of excellence.

Technique 4: Train hard, fight easy

Technique 5: Focus on who, rather than how

Technique 6: Establishing your battle rhythm and Immediate Action drills

Technique 4: Train Hard, Fight Easy

The concept of training hard to fight easy is not a new one. Elite military and law enforcement units around the world and throughout history have placed great emphasis on making training as realistic and as difficult as possible so that when the day of reckoning comes, the battle is more likely to be won. There's no substitute for regular learning, preparation, and then practice, testing your ability to perform under pressure in a safe environment.

When not deployed on kidnap negotiations, I spend my time working with businesses and organizations across all industries and sectors to develop their leadership team capability by facilitating tabletop, immersive exercises based on real kidnap-for-ransom cases. This experience replicates situations where there are significant challenges for employees, operational delivery, business viability, or even organizational reputation. Most organizations will, thankfully, never face such an ordeal for real, but "training hard" in these types of exercises quickly develops the required muscle memories (both individually and organizationally) of resilience, culture, leadership, and decision-making in uncertainty, as well as enhancing emotional intelligence and communication skills.

Being a world-class negotiator is not a solo activity. Inspirational leaders understand the importance of surrounding themselves with the best possible team to ensure success, particularly in challenging times. Just as in a kidnap or crisis situation, the person doing the actual negotiation is surrounded by other people scripting, coaching, prompting, and generally listening in for anything that the negotiator may miss. Each of these people has a core role to play in the success of the overall negotiation, which is why it's vital to identify, recruit, and train such people ahead of time.

Anticipation is power

One of the first things I do when establishing a Red Center or CMT is to sit down with the person who will be doing the actual communicating with the kidnappers so that we can anticipate together the likely challenges, issues, and threats that they may throw at us.

Anticipation is another superpower, because all highly successful people, teams, and organizations—regardless of their sector, industry, or lifestyle—preempt the likely (and not-so-likely) things that might get in the way of them progressing from A to B. This is not a case of gazing into a crystal ball. It is applying a systematic method that can be applied in any given situation by continuously reviewing and refining your systems and processes.

While anticipation may be one of your superpowers, it can also be used by others doing the same against you who are looking to identify your next move or offer. This applies equally to the boardroom, politics, sports teams, or even your kids testing the boundaries of what they can get away with.

In a kidnapping, one side (the kidnappers) will conduct extensive targeting and surveillance of the other (the hostage) before anticipating where he or she will be at a certain time and therefore the best conditions for the abduction to succeed. I was involved in the following real-life kidnapping that demonstrates this.

●··●··●

Negotiation Case File #3: Europe and Africa

He is only human. A smart and rich one, but still only human. We'll call him Philip. No matter how good or switched on, sooner or later everyone makes a mistake.

Today is the day that Philip will make his.

It is an easy mistake to turn right instead of left out of the gate and continue up the slight hill in his brand-new, company-owned white BMW. He feels safe, though. Why shouldn't he? He has made this journey hundreds of times before over the years. There is nothing to tell him that today will be any different.

He hadn't even planned on taking this trip when he woke up this morning. In fact, it wasn't even a consideration a few hours ago when he received the call while hard at work in his luxurious office on the top floor of the modern complex that houses his vast business empire.

It is almost three in the afternoon, and the late spring sun has begun its descent. For a few seconds, he squints in the glare, forcing him to lower the visor. This natural distraction is just enough for the dark pickup truck to ease itself out of the line of parked vehicles undetected and join the flow of traffic several cars back. The pickup is not alone, and for the occupants, this isn't their first rodeo. They have rehearsed this repeatedly.

They will make no mistakes today.

The white BMW leaves the dust cloud of the city behind and climbs further up into the hills, using the less used but more scenic route to the airport. His thoughts drift back to the phone call, the one he hadn't expected, but is glad he received. Knowing the winding route as well as he does, he cruises along almost on autopilot.

That is his second mistake.

People generally don't tell Philip that what he is doing is wrong, or that there may be a better way. He hasn't become one of the biggest businessmen in the region by not following his intuition. Hard-fought success has only emboldened him, and he now sits on an estimated fortune of over $200 million. He's earned it the hard way, by his fists if he had to in the early days, while relying on respectable business deals years later. That said, sometimes intuition gets in the way.

Slowing down too early for the upcoming bend in the road is his third mistake.

By the time he catches a glimpse of the pickup truck, it is only a couple of feet away from the front passenger door. There isn't time to do anything except instinctively brace for the inevitable impact, designed to shake him up rather than seriously injure or kill. For good measure, a second, identical pickup truck boxes in the BMW from behind, while a third does the same in front, cutting off any possibility of escape.

It's as if he's starring in his own movie as a haze of balaclavas and AK-47s appear, inching toward him in slow motion. He can't be sure how many, as a searing pain down his spine causes a disorienting double vision.

Regardless of how expensive a designer suit he wears, Philip will always feel and, if truth be told, look like an old street fighter who still takes care of himself. He enjoys the finer things in life but retains enough self-respect to not let himself go. He still has the presence of mind to reach for the glove compartment, where his hands grope for a small, concealed handgun. A sensible safety precaution for a man in his position.

That is his fourth mistake.

Bursts of automatic fire just inches from the BMW shatter every window, while Philip coils into a ball, wishing he could claw his way through the floor and down into the dry earth below. Anything to stop the deafening roar as he is showered in glass. It feels as though the shards have embedded themselves in his head, but before his hand can reach up and check, his head is yanked back as a strong forearm wraps itself tightly around his neck and pulls him out of the car, dragging his flailing body along the road. In one slick move, another balaclava appears and takes hold of his ankles, throwing him into one of the pickup trucks and pushing him down into the rear footwell.

Both balaclavas join him as his wrists are yanked behind his back and tied with plastic cuffs, immediately cutting into his wrists.

"F—" he begins to protest, before the coarse burlap sack sticks to his face. Sucking in a lungful of air, the dampness and smell of the material makes him gag.

Petrol.

Panic rises up, threatening to drown him in a dark sea of fear. He knows he is sinking further into it when he feels the shame of a wet patch in his crotch. A fire-cracking sound is too close for comfort, forcing him to jerk even further down in the footwell. A searing blast of heat follows, as the BMW abandoned just a few meters away is now no more. Satisfied that their job is done, the convoy of pickup trucks moves off at speed.

In the middle one, Philip considers how he has found himself in this position. The fog of confusion clouds any rational thought, but what is patently obvious is that he has just been kidnapped and thinks he is about to die, even though the sheer professionalism and efficiency of the kidnappers would suggest otherwise.

Thousands of kilometers away, I chuck a collapsible umbrella into the trash. It is useless against London rain that seems to fly like horizontal daggers. I feel the vibration of the phone in my jacket pocket, but I'm not about to dawdle in a downpour to answer it. I take refuge in the first building I come to; I could've chosen worse.

The Amba Hotel is one of the more reasonable ones in central London, situated just outside the Victoria train station, one of the busiest in England. Settling down into a cozy corner of the hotel lounge, I catch the eye of the waiter and order a double espresso. This promised to be a long stint. I press the redial button for the 24/7 operations center nestled in a discreet part of the city.

Forty-eight hours have elapsed since Philip was abducted and I received the call. The burned-out wreckage of the car had inevitably been found by local police soon after the event. But no one had heard anything from Philip or had any clue as to what had happened or where he was.

Such silence didn't bother me, because I knew this was just another tactic used by kidnappers to instill fear and control over the hostage's family. That said, I knew the immense stress and anxiety the family would be experiencing and that they would be fearing the worst. It was crucial that I reassure them quickly that kidnappers don't usually reach out straight away and that it could be days or weeks before they heard anything . . .

———————————•—•—•———————————

Before I engage in any form of negotiation, not just a kidnapping, I always run through the following three-step negotiation checklist. It only takes a few moments and it enables me to perform at a consistently high standard over a long period of time, especially when the stakes can't get any higher.

Step 1: Manage your own state

I would never walk into a negotiation without first checking my state and determining what emotion was showing up for me. I would always ask myself how I was feeling and, for example, whether there was any resistance or tension present. Everything comes down to tuning into this sensory acuity. Its importance cannot be overstated.

This is why it should be the first port of call as you open your awareness of what emotions you may be experiencing before you walk into that all-important meeting or discussion. Is it excitement, nervousness, fear, frustration, or determination, for example? Where and how is it showing up in your body? Is there tightness across your chest or shoulders, a churning in your stomach, or simply a healthy dose of tension all over? Is it lifting you up and propelling you forward rather than dragging you back and pulling you down?

From developing this awareness and acknowledging what you're feeling, you can then more accurately interpret it, such as why it might be showing up right now and what it might be drawing your attention to. Having done this, you can then take steps to interpret the needs and fears of all the other "stakeholders" involved in your meeting or negotiation. For me, this might be the family of the hostage, the local police, kidnappers, or even my fellow negotiators. Managing my own state enables me to adapt my own communication style accordingly.

Another means of bringing about an empowering state is by being mindful of where you place your focus and the meaning you give it. For example, are you seeing the situation as a major problem or seeing the opportunity within it?

Step 2: Harness your Red Center

Once you've managed your state, it's time to tap into your Red Center. As we've already discovered, this is that part of you where you can utilize a mindset and behaviors that allow you to operate at your very best, no matter what the circumstances.

One of the most effective ways of preparing your arsenal is commonly referred to in peak performance literature as "the zone" or more often as "flow." It was the Hungarian psychologist Mihaly Csikszentmihalyi who first coined the concept of "flow" and said: "By stretching your skills and reaching toward higher challenges, such a person becomes an increasingly extraordinary individual."

In *The Rise of Superman: Decoding the Science of Ultimate Human Performance*, journalist Steven Kotler builds on this idea by advocating that we seek out challenges that force us to become comfortable with being uncomfortable. Once you've identified such opportunities and overcome the initial resistance, frustration, and fear, allow the naturally produced adrenaline and cortisol to prime your body for flow state.

For me, this would usually be in the first twenty-four hours of a kidnapping, when the tidal wave of information, the raw emotion of the hostage's family and colleagues, and the pressure for me to bring order out of chaos has the potential to be overwhelming. Accepting and releasing this innate survival mechanism allowed me to override any remaining "struggle" I might have had, thereby allowing feel-good endorphins to flush through my body and create clarity, focus, and peak performance. It would also increase my ability to find creative solutions to problems, which was essential during a kidnap negotiation, particularly during the ransom-drop phase, when things were most likely to go drastically wrong.

This approach can be applied in any area of life and is often seen in sports. In fact, it can be obtained during any kind of physical activity that requires focusing attention and exerting lots of physical effort. Studies have even found that military snipers trained in a state of flow learned 230 percent faster than normal.

In a *Harvard Business Review* article, "Create a Work Environment That Fosters Flow," Kotler highlights a ten-year study conducted by McKinsey, in which top executives reported being five times more productive in flow. According to the researchers, if we could increase the time we spend in flow by 15 to 20 percent, overall workplace productivity would almost double. While this study was based on anecdotal observations over a lengthy period of time, rather than being a controlled scientific one, its results remain highly impressive, nonetheless.

So how can you train yourself to enter this flow state and harness your Red Center at will? One way is to identify "Goldilocks activities." These are found at the midpoint between boredom and anxiety, where the task is hard enough to stretch you, but not so hard it'll break you. If the challenge is too great, fear swamps your nervous system, but if it's too easy, you'll stop paying attention and give up.

With my coaching clients, for example, I emphasize to the high performers among them that they must learn that slow and steady wins this race, while those who perceive themselves to be underachievers must learn the opposite: that being uncomfortable is a sign of progress, not a reason to run away.

Step 3: Visualize success ahead of time

Once you're in a great flow state and tapped into your Red Center, the final step in your checklist before you engage with anyone is to spend a brief moment visualizing the meeting, conversation, or negotiation working out for the best. However, first you might wish to incorporate a negative visualization of the worst-case scenario occurring. While this may sound counterintuitive, it has been used as a highly effective technique for thousands of years.

It was the Stoic philosophers, such as Seneca and Marcus Aurelius, who first recommended the benefits of visualizing the negative outcomes that could arise in everyday scenarios. This would have the effect of desensitizing us to such an outcome if it occurred. We would also be more likely to stay calm and respond appropriately rather than emotionally.

This is something I regularly did during tense kidnap negotiations. Not because I'm a negative person—far from it. By asking myself and the rest of the crisis management team questions such as, "What's the worst thing that could happen with this negotiation?" or "What would it be like if x, y, or z happened?" and "How might we prevent it from happening, or if it did, what could we do about it?"

Doing this enables you to identify blind spots in individuals, teams, and across organizations. It also prevents naive optimism from prevailing. In other words, plan for the best, but prepare for the worst. It was the legendary former heavyweight champion Mike Tyson, who, reflecting on the collapse of his fortune, said, "If you're not humble, life will visit humbleness upon you."

For you, this might be visualizing a situation in which a key client pulls out of a complicated and lucrative deal you've been working on for months, or perhaps your family holiday is delayed extensively due to bad weather. In a kidnapping, I wouldn't just have a Plan B ready, but a Plan C and D as well, just in case. That way, everyone's expectations were managed and we were as prepared as we could be for all eventualities. And while it's impossible to plan for every eventuality, by developing such an approach, everyone has certainty and reassurance that we'll find a way through, no matter what occurs.

Once you've completed a negative visualization and considered the worst-case scenarios, you can move on to thinking about what success looks, sounds, and feels like to you. It helps to know your desired outcome ahead of time for every meeting, phone call, or conversation. For example, if I go into any negotiation seeking anything other than success, I can guarantee this will leak out in my language, tone, body posture, even the energy or vibe that I give off. Hence, the importance of visualizing success in your own mind before a single word is spoken.

It will also activate the reticular activating system (RAS) in your brain, which controls what you focus on and perceive in your consciousness, essentially acting as a gatekeeper of information. A classic everyday example of this is if you decide you want to buy a red 4×4 vehicle, then you will likely see a lot more red 4×4s as you go about your day; not because there are more, it's just that your brain knows what to focus on and give attention to.

- How can you apply your own version of this checklist into your daily life?
- What would all areas of your life look, sound, and feel like if you were able to perform this quick check-in with yourself before a meeting, sending an important email, or making a phone call?

There's an old saying that slow is smooth, and smooth is fast. By taking the time to slow down to run through a checklist, you will be able to move much more quickly and easily when it counts and the pressure is mounting. This is because, when you walk into the boardroom or a meeting to engage in a serious conversation or deliver an important presentation, you've got to be able to perform at your best right from the outset. There's no room for a warmup once you've started. That must be done way before you get to the starting line.

When I walk into the kitchen of the hostage's family for the first time, I only get one chance to establish credibility and trust. If I mess up, it's nearly impossible to recover. I've known negotiators to make just one offhand comment or allow their focus to drop, albeit for a very short moment, but it was enough for them to be on the next plane home and a replacement sent out. It didn't happen very often because of the intense selection and training process to become a kidnap negotiator in the first place. But when it did, it only made the replacement's job twice as hard, as if it weren't challenging enough in the first place.

<hr>

Meanwhile, back on the case with Philip . . .

The local police were rapidly moving into gear, saying they were going to hold press conferences. I knew I had to move fast, as this was the exact opposite of what we wanted or needed.

Ordinarily, raising the profile of the hostage only serves to increase their perceived value in the eyes of the kidnappers, who in turn hold out for more money. Each day a hostage spends held captive increases the risk to their life. In this case, however, the kidnappers clearly knew who the victim was and how much he was worth. That said, just because somebody is worth a certain amount doesn't mean that worth can easily be converted into hard cash in a bag and dropped off at a given location without being detected. The hostage's worth may be tied up in a company, for example, and then suddenly it becomes difficult, if not impossible, to legally liquidate assets in time.

The clock was ticking.

——————————— ● ● ● ———————————

One of the things a good kidnap negotiator will do when they first meet either the family or company is to talk through the likely scenarios of how the negotiation will develop. This is based on the extensive collective experience of the team working hard behind the scenes to support the negotiator, such as analysts or other negotiators. During one of the early meetings, the negotiator will sit down with the CMT and establish the five most likely challenges, threats, and questions that they're likely to receive from the kidnappers. This is sometimes referred to as the Bunch of Fives.

Doing so buys them breathing space and thinking time, so when that comment or question is raised, it doesn't take anyone by surprise. This allows the negotiator to respond coolly and objectively, rather than stumbling and reacting, potentially eroding any trust and credibility that had been established with the hostage-takers.

Consider the positive impact of spending time either by yourself or with your team or family to discuss, plan, implement, and review your own version of a Bunch of Fives, focusing on one of the areas each week. Then when you've gone through all five, go back to the beginning and redo them. This then becomes a never-ending process of anticipation and improvement. Most importantly, it means you'll always be able to stay one step ahead and preempt all the likely things that will prevent you from succeeding in whatever form of negotiation you're engaged in.

Consider using the following as a template. For each of the points below, ask: What are the top three to five most likely challenges or obstacles that could impact you or your business? How can you overcome them to be the best communicator you can be?

1. **Outcome.** Establish exactly where you are and what you want to achieve. Is it planning a wedding or moving to a new house, or overseeing the acquisition of another company? What is the result you're after, and what is the plan to achieve it?

2. **Sales and marketing.** Even if you don't officially "sell" or "market" in your role, you'll be doing so in reality, whether you realize it or not. You could be selling and marketing yourself, your ideas, brand, or beliefs as well as any professional product or service you offer.

3. **People and processes.** Who do you need on your team? Who are the key people around you who can support you in your negotiations? Identify those people who seek to "blow out your flame," rather than champion you at every opportunity. They will provide you with the opportunity to establish boundaries and create a healthy distance between you.

4. **Financials.** Look at your numbers. Do you need to review your cash flow or budget? Who do you need to support you with this? What would a clear dashboard of financial data give you that you currently don't have?

5. **Government, legal, policy.** What are some of the most challenging shifts in legislation, government, or company policy that could have a disproportionate impact on your life or business? Anticipating these considerations will give you the confidence to engage in any form of negotiation with a high degree of certainty of success, no matter what happens.

As you work your way through your Bunch of Fives, always look for ways in which you can train yourself or your team, as well as how you can best prepare for, mitigate, or avoid any negative impact. If recent years have shown us anything, it's the importance of remaining agile and constantly reviewing the efficiency and effectiveness of systems and processes. Consider utilizing a Red Team to help you with this. We will cover this in more detail in the next section.

Technique 5: Focus on Who, Rather Than How

In his book *Good to Great*, the business writer Jim Collins argues that the success of any team is usually down to having "the right people on the right bus, sitting in the right seats." Collins goes on to describe how you can have some brilliant people working in a team or organization, yet if they're not placed in the best role for them, based on their suitability, preferences, and skills, it will only end badly for everyone in the long run. When seeking to identify who sits where, there are three powerful questions that can be asked of the individual. These apply equally to performing roles within a negotiation, hiring new staff, or in your personal and intimate relationships.

1. Can they do the job? (i.e., technically. Are they "qualified"?)

2. Will they do the job well in the long term? (Is it in their inherent nature?)

3. Are they a good fit in the team? (Do they share similar values and outlook?)

Can they do the job?

Usually this is easily answered, because the person wouldn't even find themselves in contention for the job, business partnership, or intimate relationship if they weren't technically capable or compatible.

Will they do the job (long term)?

This question is more challenging. Imagine a people-focused, highly driven sales executive being asked to go and work in the accounts department, filing paperwork and completing spreadsheets all day. Could they do the job? Probably. Will they do the job? If they had to. But would they do it well, long term? The answer is likely to be a "no." Why? Because such a role is not playing to their strengths and skills. It's not in their inherent core nature. It doesn't mean the accounting role is any less important than the sales one, just that this person's skill set is better focused in a different role more suited to them.

The same applies to negotiation. While we can all do it, and are doing so every day, when it comes to selecting a team to either support or conduct negotiations alongside you, you need the right people in the right seats. That's what this book is all about—giving everyone the knowledge, skills, and strategies that they can then refine and make their own with practice.

In a relationship context, for example, one person may be an outgoing extrovert who loves to travel and seek out adventure, while the other person is more introverted and likes to stay at home and have a quieter life. At first, physical chemistry will override these differences and the other's persona will seem playful, exciting, creative, or calming. But after a while, this could turn into irritation, frustration, and resentment. It doesn't mean that as individuals they won't be the perfect match for somebody else, though.

Are they a good fit in the team?

While the person may be capable, compatible, and look as if they are suitable for the long term, the final deciding question that will determine which seat or even which bus they need to be on is, "Are they a good team fit?"

Do they fit in with the organizational culture or other person's values and beliefs? It has been well established that people like people who are like themselves. Can I work with this person? Can I trust them? Will they have the resilience and positive mindset to persevere when the going gets tough? Will they have the emotional intelligence and sensory acuity to fit in with the rest of the team?

Before you can build your ideal negotiating team, you must first understand how your attitude and subsequently your communication can impact another person's behavior and therefore their communication.

As mentioned earlier, when you negotiate, whatever you focus on and the meaning you give it will affect how you feel and, subsequently, the actions you then take. This, in turn, will affect how the other person perceives

FIGURE 2-1

An inside job

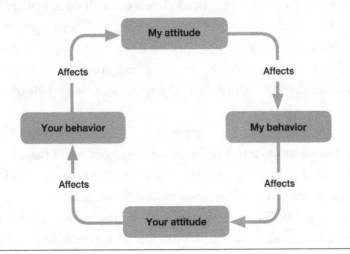

you and how they respond. This can be seen in the diagram of the "Betari's box" concept, which illustrates how your attitude and behavior affect the attitude and behavior of the people you interact with (figure 2-1).

Imagine that you're feeling frustrated because a work colleague hasn't completed an important task you requested. When you talk to them, your voice may become louder, more direct, and maybe even abrupt. The other person might then respond to what they subconsciously perceive as a threat or criticism by raising their voice, going silent, or into a defensive mode. They may even refuse to engage at all.

If you are going into a negotiation that may involve conflict, interrupt this cycle by first managing your own attitude and getting into a more beneficial emotional state. Otherwise, it's likely that both sides of the negotiation will remain stuck in a loop, with no one making any meaningful progress.

You may also have a little voice in your head prompting you to respond in the unhelpful way you've been cognitively conditioned to do. That little voice is nothing more than that though. It's in your head and is based on your own characteristic fears, values, beliefs, and presumptions about others, usually based on the meaning you've given painful or pleasurable experiences from your past. All decisions you make are controlled by these values and beliefs, including the quality of all your relationships, both personally and professionally, and how well you communicate within them.

Building your negotiation team

To be an effective leader and negotiator, it is essential to understand the different types of people in your team and which seats on the bus they need to sit on to allow them to thrive, contribute, and play to their strengths, particularly when effective communication is required or during an important negotiation.

One of the very first things I do when notified of a new kidnapping is to clarify and verify with the client who is taking responsibility for establishing a CMT. This is the person who will be leading the key personnel and helping to bring about the safe and timely release and recovery of the hostage. The CMT usually consists of functional decision-makers for key areas, such as legal, finance, HR and well-being, security, etc.

Once I know the answer, I can then begin offering advice and recommending Immediate Actions to get us into the best possible place to weather the storm we're about to experience. This ensures that the CMT is made up of the right people in the right roles. Sometimes, the answer to this question was less than reassuring. Instead, a number of people were all attempting to take control, with nothing actually being achieved except an unfortunate display of unhealthy egos competing for significance.

When faced with your own challenge, crossroads, or crisis, if you can quickly form your own version of a CMT, ideally with no more than a handful of carefully chosen people, all with clearly defined roles and responsibilities, it enables highly efficient and effective discussions and decision-making to take place. In other words, surround yourself with those people whose opinions you trust and who can be relied on to support you when the going gets tough.

While the CMT is most likely to be an established and fully trained team within a large corporate organization, it could also be you and your family sitting down around the kitchen table to talk through a particular challenge or issue affecting you all. No matter the size or composition, the key factor is that everyone gets a voice, with the "CMT chair" having the final say.

Selecting a negotiator

Whoever is in charge, particularly in a corporate or hierarchical organization, often likes to do the talking in a crisis. In the high-stakes world of kidnap negotiation, allowing ego to take over the communication will usually get the hostage killed. Also, if the CEO or chair of the CMT is already communicating with the kidnappers, we don't have any room to maneuver or slow down the process by telling the kidnappers we're "checking with the boss," which buys us valuable thinking time. They may also want to appear decisive and then agree to something under pressure. This makes our job of getting the hostage back even more difficult than it already is.

In a kidnap case, one of my roles was to advise the client or family on how to select, coach, and guide the person who is most suitable to be the negotiator or the "communicator," as they're known in the Red Center. This is a crucial role, as they'll be the only link between us and the kidnappers. If they screw up and say the wrong thing, or the right thing but in the wrong tone, they can easily put the hostage in greater danger. What we're looking to do is to separate the physical negotiation with the bad guys from the actual decision-making process about how much ransom to pay and when. This separation gives us valuable breathing space and time.

This is why negotiators are deliberately not decision-makers during a crisis. While they are more than capable of making decisions, they need to keep a safety net in place that enables them to delay and buy more time if required to face down the kidnappers' demands.

This concept of separating the negotiation and decision-making roles can equally apply to other areas of your life, such as buying a new house or a car. Even if it's just you. I'm sure you've all used something similar to "Let me sleep on it" or "Let me think about it." All you're doing here is separating the process, to buy yourself time in order to make a rational, objective decision that is not driven by raw emotion or ego. This applies even though human beings often make decisions emotionally and then justify them rationally afterward. Think of it as "commander's command, while negotiators negotiate," and never mix the two.

Choose wisely when selecting your CMT, because, as the timeless adage goes, "You become who you spend most of your time with." Even if you don't have anyone else to help form this team, you can still take on the role yourself. The most pressing issue, however, for anyone assuming the role of CMT Chair, even if it's just you, is to take 100 percent responsibility for the situation and to accept the reality of what is being faced. This awareness and acknowledgment will reassure everyone, not least yourself.

At the same time, you've already seen how being calm is contagious and essential for the leader in order to provide clear direction and empower the team to deliver. The most effective leaders and negotiators also avoid burying their heads in the sand and are always expecting the best, yet preparing for the worst. Nor do they avoid asking (and answering) those difficult questions that arise in such situations.

Creating a Red Team

Red Teaming is a modern-day version of the old Vatican official, otherwise known as the "devil's advocate," whose role was to discredit candidates for sainthood. Today, a Red Team is a group of professional sceptics and saboteurs whose primary role is to test the defenses of your building, IT system, or even your argument. This can be particularly effective when preparing for an important negotiation.

National security expert Micah Zenko, in his book *Red Team: How to Succeed by Thinking Like the Enemy*, describes the concept as: "Seeking to better understand the interests, intentions and capabilities of ... potential competitors. Red Teaming includes simulations, vulnerability probes and alternative analysis ... also helping institutions in competitive environments and anticipate potential threats ahead of the next special operations raid, malicious cyber-attack or corporate merger."

It is one thing instructing a Red Team to creatively test your defenses, but it requires even greater courage to accept and implement their recommendations. Failure to do so can have catastrophic consequences, though, not just to the outcome of your negotiation but also in shifting the course of history for generations. An example of this was contained in a statement made before a public hearing into the events of 9/11 in the United States. Those present in the public hearings were told that the Federal Aviation Authority (FAA) had been warned by an FAA Red Team about vulnerabilities in airport security that could easily be exploited by terrorists, yet the findings were ignored by the FAA leadership.

When leaders have the courage to accept a Red Team's findings, however, the impact can set the better course of history, as shown by the multiple independent analyses and simulations instrumental in the successful 2011 raid to kill Osama Bin Laden.

Equally in business, Red Teams used ahead of major decisions, particularly in relation to a competitor's new strategy or product launch, for example, can dismantle the rigid thinking and fixed mindsets of executives and reap the rewards of their courage.

In your own tough negotiations, consider building on the Bunch of Fives technique and utilize a Red Team to identify vulnerabilities, challenge assumptions, and anticipate threats impacting your life or business. Essentially, you want them to think and act like the enemy, even though they're actually the good guys.

Technique 6: Establishing Your Battle Rhythm and Immediate Action Drills

How are you going to respond when time is of the essence to strike a deal? The initial response to a challenging situation, crisis, or adversity should be decisive, with an intent to bring as much clarity and perspective to what is usually a fog of chaos and uncertainty. This could be that moment when you receive a phone call, an email, or have a conversation you know will change everything in an instant. It is about consciously responding to events in an optimal way, rather than allowing yourself to merely react. This section will cover ways in which you can do so.

Ultimately, how you respond in the first few moments of any given situation will undoubtedly impact how it could end. In a kidnapping, it is vital that the hostage's family or organization gets a grip early and establishes a supportive team to help them navigate through the situation and toward success; all without placing the hostages at risk of further harm or death. In order to successfully achieve this, it's imperative your negotiation team aren't burned out and unable to perform when the crunch time comes.

Establishing a sustainable battle rhythm and routine

Depending where in the world the kidnapping occurs and who is responsible, along with the profile of the hostages, bringing about a successful resolution can take days, weeks, months, and, occasionally, even years. This is why I always prepare the client for the long haul. Yes, we may get a lucky break and the hostage escapes, or the kidnappers suddenly decide keeping the hostage requires too much effort and isn't worth the risk to themselves, but this is very rare. Usually, it requires vast amounts of patience and resilience over a long period of time. To keep everyone in the CMT fresh and capable of thinking and acting with clarity and focus, it's crucial to establish something called a "battle rhythm."

There is a saying, "Show me your routine and I'll show you your success." A battle rhythm is just like a routine. Not the kind of routine that you only follow when things are easy and everything is going in your favor. Any fool can do that. It's following it even when you don't want to and when every story and disempowering belief you can think of is screaming at you to not show up today.

Establishing a consistent routine is fundamental to the successful resolution of any form of crisis, challenge, or conflict, just as it is to a kidnapping or when you simply want to get the best out of yourself. Why so much emphasis on routine? Because routines create habits. Habits create character, and character creates your life. It's through rituals, routines, and habits that you ultimately forge your identity.

The most effective leaders and negotiators I've either worked with or coached had both a mental and physical routine they followed, no matter what. It's the one thing they refuse to negotiate with themselves. It's what got them to the top and enabled them to thrive once there. There is no set formula or one way of doing it, as it has to work for you, in your circumstances.

Think long term

However focused and committed the CMT is in negotiating the release of the hostage, life has to go on during the period in which they're held. Businesses still need to be run, and families need to go about their day-to-day activities as much as possible. If we don't establish a routine, our very own battle rhythm, then people are quickly overwhelmed and suffer burnout and eventually break down. Not establishing such a routine can potentially lead to tragic consequences, as it hinders the negotiation process and ultimately increases the threat to the hostages.

Now back to the case file . . .

With Philip now taken hostage, his cousin, as de facto head of the family, took it upon himself to be the chair of the CMT, chief negotiator, and ultimate decision-maker, against all advice to the contrary. One person taking on all these roles is fraught with danger, but the cousin initially fared well and seemed to relish the attention.

He took everything in his stride and appeared to see this as an opportunity to showcase his talents now that he wasn't living in the shadow of his cousin. However, progress in the negotiations then quickly began unraveling, as he continued to ignore all our advice to establish a battle rhythm and call window. He made matters even worse by refusing to use a brand-new mobile phone, also known as a "clean" phone, to communicate with the kidnappers.

The purpose of doing this is so that the only people in the world who know the new number, other than ourselves, are the kidnappers. If you stick with your existing phone, what happens is that every SMS, WhatsApp, email notification, or phone call received from anyone is immediately thought to be from the kidnappers.

Inevitably, it wasn't long before the cousin became a physical and emotional wreck, incapable of any effective negotiating, decision-making, or leadership of the CMT. Even more worryingly, he also refused the pleas of his family to take a break and to follow professional advice. This refusal to establish a battle rhythm, or simply to get sufficient rest, impacted his ability to communicate under pressure, which in turn almost led to his cousin being killed. After weeks of tense negotiations and having had no sleep for several days, he ended up threatening the kidnappers with revenge, which resulted in them calmly responding that they were going to kill the hostage and the family would never see him again, before abruptly ending the phone call.

Three long months of painful silence followed without any contact from the kidnappers. But because the cousin had refused to use the clean phone, he continued to receive plenty of notification pings and calls all day long from just about everyone else. Each time, his heart would soar in anticipation of it being from Philip or the kidnappers, only to be crushed. All this could have been avoided.

Resentment from the wider family grew and it became almost too much for him. This was one of the most challenging "crises within a crisis" I had ever experienced. Eventually, the cousin ceded control of not only the phone itself, but also all the negotiations too. Not long afterward, Philip was released and reunited with his family.

What does your daily routine look like?

Having debriefed many hostages upon their release, what is noticeable is that they all share similar stories about how they survived and the importance having a routine had on their mental well-being and survival.

So what does your daily routine look like? Does it involve some form of exercise or mobility work? Maybe journaling, meditation, or cold showers are your thing? It can be whatever enables you to thrive, grow, and develop as an individual and as a member of a team. Importantly, it must be easy to apply and maintain. Consistency and longevity are the guiding principles.

Slow down to speed up

Once the small CMT has been established in the Red Center, with the right people sitting in the right seats and a dedicated phone line set up to speak with the kidnappers, I always urge them, whether it's the family or a company, to take a breath and simply pause. Gather your thoughts, take stock of what has happened. This allows valuable thinking time to work through the various negotiation strategy options in a calm manner.

It also provides a stable platform from which to move, decide, and take action quickly, if required, rather than feeling pressured and out of control. Effectively, you want to be buying time. You're not necessarily talking about a long period here; just a few moments to breathe, gather your thoughts, and run through options, enabling you to come up with some form of strategy that supports the decision-making. Remember, it hasn't got to be perfect. You just need to make a decision. The positive effect of such a pause can be immense, as it creates that small gap between stimulus and response where you can make decisions rationally.

Creating your own Immediate Action drill

You don't have to wait too long these days before someone will happily tell you how they were "triggered" by so-and-so or such-and-such. You've probably experienced such a trigger yourself. Whenever you find yourself experiencing these moments, it's useful to have some way of interrupting the usually negative and disempowering emotions that follow.

But what do we mean when we refer to being "triggered"? It's essentially when something unresolved from your past shows up in the present moment. Often your reaction will appear disproportionate to the situation itself and, despite knowing this intellectually at the time, you still find yourself experiencing powerful emotions and subsequently indulging in unhelpful behavior.

What Is a Trigger?

There might be an old metal tin that belongs to your partner sitting on top of the refrigerator that used to contain sweets and other treats for the kids. One day, you notice that it's empty and, as your kids don't really eat sweets any more, you move the tin and use it for something else. When your partner notices this, they experience an extreme emotion accompanied by a reaction that appears "over the top" to you. You can't believe they've reacted like this to an old tin.

But by maintaining curiosity and applying the adage, "First seek to understand, before being understood," you'll realize that it's actually got nothing to do with the tin. By empathizing and utilizing your emotional intelligence, you may discover that your partner previously had their property taken away from them, or perhaps it was disrespected or badly treated. Imagine an old wound that hasn't healed properly and each trigger merely reopens it.

In the next chapter, we'll go into more detail about how such triggers can physically impact our bodies and can interfere with our ability to negotiate effectively, particularly during crises and other challenging times. We'll also learn techniques for how you can overcome them. But for now, every time you find yourself communicating with someone and you become triggered, consider the following:

1. Interrupt the pattern by shifting your focus, the language you're using, or even your body by standing up or going for a walk outside.

2. Refuse to allow a negative thought or feeling to take hold for more than ninety seconds. It's perfectly normal to experience these,

particularly in times of overwhelming stress, but it's another thing to stay there, allowing the stories to play on a loop inside your head.

3. Ask empowering questions of yourself, such as: What else could this mean? Where is the gift in this situation? What is the opportunity or learning for me? What am I not seeing here? How can this enable me to grow?

What if the kidnappers call now?

Part of the Immediate Action drill and the setting up of the Red Center or CMT at the start of a kidnap negotiation is to ask the question, "What if the kidnappers call now?" This question was always at the forefront of my mind and one I would frequently ask the client. I would then consider asking the following questions:

- Are you ready to take their call?

- Is the recording device set up and working so you can play back the calls to make sure you don't misunderstand what is said or agreed to?

- Do you know what you're going to say?

- Are you comfortable with the script and prompts?

Essentially, these questions are about ensuring everyone is ready to face whatever happens. It is not a onetime checklist exercise, though. Throughout the whole negotiation process, you need to ask the same questions continuously.

So, when the call comes in, whatever your version of "the call" is in your life or business, are you ready to get a grip on it and take ownership, responsibility, and the Immediate Action required?

Having utilized the power of anticipation and your Bunch of Fives, you're now ready to also ask yourself the following questions:

1. What is the worst that can happen right now?

2. Are you prepared for it?

3. Do you have the right mindset, psychology, tools, strategies, and resources? If so, great. If not, why not? Let's do something about it.

Establishing a call window

In every kidnap negotiation, one of our initial tactics is to enforce a set period of time in which we will be available to speak with the kidnappers. This is known as the "call window." This simply means persuading the kidnappers to stick to the agreed times; for example, between 2 p.m. and 5 p.m. every afternoon, when our phone will be switched on and we'll be available to negotiate with them. For the remaining twenty-one hours each day, that phone will be switched off.

This is important, as it gives us an element of control over the negotiations. It also allows the CMT to get into a steady and manageable battle rhythm; time for daily exercise, eating the right foods, and getting decent-quality rest and sleep periods.

It also gives the CMT time to discuss the various options and challenges in the case. These can include ensuring that a decent level of support is being offered to the families of the hostages and considering any crisis communication issues, such as leaks to the media. It also allows us an opportunity to plan and overcome the not-inconsiderable logistical task of getting all the ransom money together before establishing how we will transport it safely to the kidnappers without being discovered.

The call window works in the kidnappers' favor too, as their communicator might have to travel some distance to make the call to ensure he's not making it from the camp or stronghold where they're holding the hostage.

In your own life, blocking out time every day for yourself is invaluable. Whether that means turning your phone off, shutting down your laptop, or even leaving it on the desk as you go for a lunchtime walk. It positively reinforces your own sense of self-worth, that you really do matter and that you take your self-care and mental wellness seriously. Putting the "oxygen mask" on yourself first enables you to take on any challenge, issue, or project with grace, calm, and ease. The same applies equally to your team or family. By going first as a leader and demonstrating it, you are signaling consent that it's okay for them to do the same. Imagine how collectively united and unstoppable you and your team could be when you establish your very own battle rhythm.

A Negotiation Checkup

Let's do a quick negotiation check.

- What aspects of your negotiation arsenal need improvement the most? Do you find yourself quick to judge? Or do you frequently offer other people advice and attempt to problem-solve, rather than listening to them with an open, empathetic, and curious mind?

- Why is that? Is it because you struggle to negotiate with others who may be displaying strong emotions?

- What challenges have you experienced as a result? Perhaps your relationships aren't as strong as they could be because people no longer confide in you or come to you for support because they don't feel truly listened to?

- What are some of the ways your life could be improved as a result of becoming a world-class negotiator? Could it be that you're no longer triggered by what other people say to you? Are you now able to choose a far more deliberate and reasonable response, rather than your old habitual, knee-jerk aggressive reaction?

- How will it help you in negotiating a raise, talking to your spouse or kids, or even improving how you talk to yourself? Perhaps it will give you greater confidence and certainty to listen more effectively. Or, you are now better at articulating your wants, needs, and boundaries clearly.

This might feel slightly awkward or unnatural at first. In everyday life, most of us just negotiate without giving it the attention it deserves. You don't usually take the time to step back and think long and hard about how you talk to people and the desired outcomes of your conversations. By doing so and practicing often, you will be well on your way to being a better negotiator, as repetition is not only a key skill but also the mother of mastery.

Chapter Summary

To succeed in any form of negotiation, preparation is key. If you consistently apply the following techniques, you'll be able to approach challenging circumstances with focus, clarity, and calmness.

TRAIN HARD, FIGHT EASY: Regular learning, preparation, and practice in a safe environment are crucial for performing under pressure. By taking the time to slow down and apply these tools, techniques, and strategies, you can move quickly and easily when it counts and the pressure is mounting. Remember, slow is smooth, smooth is fast.

USE A NEGOTIATION CHECKLIST: Before any meeting, phone call, email, or conversation, follow this three-step negotiation checklist to triumph every time. This ensures that you are adequately prepared and increases your chances of success:

1. **Manage your own state.** Before important meetings or negotiations, become aware of your emotions and physical sensations. Understand why you're feeling a certain way and adapt your communication style accordingly. Be mindful of where you focus your attention. Is it the opportunities within a situation or dwelling on the problem?

2. **Harness your own Red Center.** Tap into the part of you that allows you to operate at your best, regardless of the circumstances. Seek out challenges that push you out of your comfort zone and activate

your flow state. A willingness to embrace increasing discomfort is a sign of progress.

3. **Plan for the best while preparing for the worst.** Spend time visualizing a positive outcome for your meetings or negotiations. Simultaneously, consider worst-case scenarios and develop plans to prevent or address possible obstacles. This helps desensitize you to potential negative outcomes and ensures that you're prepared for any situation.

ESTABLISH A BUNCH OF FIVES: Identify the top five challenges, risks, and questions you are likely to encounter in a negotiation. By anticipating these and preparing to overcome them, you can stay one step ahead and increase your chances of success.

FOCUS ON WHO, RATHER THAN HOW: Make sure the right people are sitting in the right seats on the right bus. When assembling a team or identifying roles within a negotiation, consider whether individuals can do the job, do it well in the long term, and fit well within the team. Match people's strengths and skills with the right roles to maximize their contribution.

MANAGE YOUR ATTITUDE AND BEHAVIOR: Use Batari's Box concept to help you recognize that your attitude and behavior can influence the attitude and behavior of others. In negotiations involving conflict, manage your attitude to break the cycle and make progress.

SEPARATE NEGOTIATION FROM DECISION-MAKING: During crises or important negotiations, separate the communications from the decision-making. This allows you to make rational, objective decisions without being held hostage by your emotions.

ESTABLISH A BATTLE RHYTHM AND ROUTINE: Develop a consistent routine or battle rhythm to maintain clarity, focus, and resilience during challenging situations. Following a routine helps create habits that lead to success and prevents burnout or becoming overwhelmed.

HAVE AN IMMEDIATE ACTION DRILL: Develop your own powerful Immediate Action drill to extract yourself from situations where you find yourself triggered and emotionally hijacked by a pressing need to rescue the deal or conversation:

1. **Interrupt the pattern.** Shift your focus, the language you're using, or even your body by standing up or going for a walk outside.

2. **Refuse to allow negative thoughts or feelings to take hold for more than ninety seconds.** It's perfectly normal to experience these, particularly in times of overwhelming stress, but it's another thing to allow the stories to play on a loop inside your head.

3. **Ask empowering questions.** What else could this mean? Where is the gift in this situation? What is the opportunity or learning for me? What am I not seeing here? How can this enable me to grow?

ESTABLISH REGULAR CALL WINDOWS: Blocking out time every day for yourself is invaluable. This provides you with an element of control over negotiations. It allows for a steady and manageable battle rhythm, such as daily exercise, sleep, eating the right foods, and getting decent rest. This might look like turning your phone off or shutting down your laptop to go for a lunchtime walk.

Key Takeaways

1. Use your negotiation checklist before every meeting, phone call, email, or conversation.

2. Get your team sitting in the right seats on the right bus.

3. Schedule time for yourself during the day to relax and recharge to prevent burnout or becoming overwhelmed.

CHAPTER THREE

Practical Psychology to Influence Any Negotiation

So far, we've covered the importance of developing your mindset and preparing yourself and your team for negotiating. In this chapter, we'll go behind the curtain and look at some of the psychology that underpins what we do. You will learn the practical tools, grounded in neuroscience and forged in real-world negotiations, that you can apply in your everyday life, enabling you to win every time. Specifically, we will cover the following:

Technique 7: First moves: Establishing your communication strategy

Technique 8: How it all works: The science behind negotiation

Technique 9: Proactive listening, establishing rapport, trust-based influence

Technique 7: First Moves: Establishing Your Communication Strategy

In a kidnapping, the bad guys will explore all avenues to spread confusion and negotiate with as many members of the victim's family or colleagues as they can in order to obtain as much money as possible. This is why it was my job to regain control of the message being negotiated and how it was being conveyed. In this section, we'll cover how you can learn to negotiate more effectively and develop your ability to influence and persuade people using key aspects of kidnap negotiation.

By taking such an approach in your day-to-day life, particularly when faced with stressful or challenging situations, you will be able to remain mindful of what you say and how you say it, thereby avoiding the wrong message being conveyed, which could jeopardize both individual and organizational reputations, viability, and profitability. Thankfully, there is a clear path to doing this effectively, which we'll explore in this chapter.

In a kidnap case, it is also my job as the "response consultant" to advise the client or family on how to select, coach, and guide the person most suitable to be the "communicator." This is a crucial role, as they'll be the only link between us and the kidnappers. If they screw up and say the wrong thing, or the right thing but in the wrong tone, they can easily put the hostage in greater danger.

The first place to start is refining what you're going to say by having clarity of message. This involves drafting a communication strategy and a script in the Red Center where you first work out what outcome you want to achieve in each call. Only then do we want to think about what we're actually going to say. Focusing on this "scripting" enables the negotiator to convey a clear message that will have the greatest impact and influence on the recipient. This is, of course, a constant balancing act between communicating effectively and sounding too polished and rehearsed, which might raise the suspicions of the kidnappers.

When that initial call from the kidnappers does come in, I have no more than thirty seconds to achieve my objectives. They might include the following:

- Acknowledge and reassure the kidnappers that we're taking them seriously.

- Make clear that we want to resolve this as quickly and safely as possible.

- Remind the kidnappers that they, and they alone, are responsible for the safety and welfare of the hostages until they're safely released and recovered.

- Obtain a "proof of life" that the hostages are alive.

While the tone of your voice is important in everyday communication, in a kidnap-for-ransom negotiation, it's even more so. You're usually talking to someone thousands of miles away in the middle of a jungle, ocean, or desert, with the conversation taking place over either a satellite phone (if you're lucky) or a disposable mobile phone—the very places mobile phone companies aren't too concerned about when thinking about their reception coverage. What this sounds like on a call is lots of static interference or "white noise," multiple call disconnections, and more "Sorry, can you repeat that please?" than I care to remember. That's why every call counts and there is no time to waste. It is vital to know what you want to say (and why) and how you're going to achieve it before you begin negotiating.

To further minimize any confusion or chaos orchestrated by the kidnappers, it's imperative to always seek to narrow their options by limiting communications to one voice, one number, and one message. This means they will only ever hear one voice speaking to them on the same phone number and giving one consistent message, rather than lots of people, all saying something different. And, once you're speaking on one number with one voice, you want to have one message, because if you start contradicting yourself and not following through on what you say or being inconsistent in your messaging and your communication, you could raise the conflict levels and diminish your credibility.

Before we delve into the practical communication tools and techniques you can begin to apply to your everyday lives, it's worth spending a little time examining their purpose and finding out why they are so effective. But first, let's get curious and explore why it is that you react, feel, and communicate the way you do.

Technique 8: How It All Works: The Science Behind Negotiation

Think of a time when you received a stressful phone call or were called into your manager's office. Or that time you heard a strange noise behind you when you were walking home in the dark from the train station. Behind the scenes, your body is dumping a huge amount of powerful chemicals into your system as it quickly works out whether it needs to be in fight, flight, or freeze mode. Managing and regulating your response to this onslaught of chemicals is one of the most beneficial things you can master if you want to become a world-class negotiator.

Fight, flight, or freeze

When we are triggered and overwhelmed with stress, the amygdala is activated, that part of our brains designed to warn us of life-threatening danger back when we were fighting saber-toothed tigers. At such times, the amygdala releases powerful chemicals including adrenaline and cortisol, which pump through our bodies to protect us from perceived danger and provoke intense emotions to make us act quickly. Unfortunately, this natural response primes our brains to look for what's wrong in the situation, rather than what's right.

What is more, the amygdala doesn't only release these chemicals in our bodies in response to physical danger. It does the same when we have a stressful conversation. Then, if you focus too much on your stress, your body carries on releasing cortisol, leading to serious health issues such as a suppressed immune system and increased blood pressure. Another side effect of this chemical response is hyperarousal, which is characterized by excessive activation of your nervous system, leading to emotions such as anger and anxiety, both of which are not what you want to be experiencing during a tense negotiation. Mastering this takes practice.

The psychiatrist Aaron Beck coined the term *negative automatic thoughts* (NATs) to highlight how conscious or unconscious NATs involuntarily cause unwanted negative emotions. One of your many negotiation powers lies in your ability to reframe and change the meaning you give to your NATs. The more you can achieve this, the more your brain will begin to rewire itself, and controlling your response in stressful situations will become easier.

Own your emotions

We often refer to that part of our brain responsible for our fight-or-flight response as our "reptilian" or "lizard" brain. This is a common misunderstanding that originates from the popular, but now largely superseded, triune brain concept, first theorized by neuroscientist Paul MacLean in the 1960s. MacLean argued that the brain consists of three parts (hence, triune)—the reptilian, the limbic, and the cortex, each of which developed separately over the course of our evolution as a species. The thinking around the interrelationships between these three centers has changed since MacLean's day, but it is worth outlining the basics of his theory here so that we can understand a little better the current thinking on what is going on inside our bodies during stressful situations.

Reptilian: This is layer one, thought to be responsible for all the everyday regulatory, housekeeping stuff to keep your bodies functioning, such as body temperature regulation and hormone production, without you even being aware of it.

Limbic: Layer two. Thought to be the source of your emotional responses, such as fear, hyperarousal, sexual desire, and anxiety. It was said to activate your so-called reptilian brain with increased heart rate and pupil dilation, for example; not because of a sudden change in your body's regulatory function, but through a shift in emotions.

Cortex: Layer three. The control panel for your impulses and emotions, responsible for long-term planning, language, and reason, and with the potential to control the emotive limbic part. It's your cortex that interprets your experience and provides an emotional response. This is why you can watch events on the television news unfolding on the other side of the planet and your reptilian brain may cause you to feel upset about it. Layer one was thought to talk to layer two, which talks to layer three and vice versa.

Previously, it was believed that the limbic (emotions) influences your abstract cognitive (cortex), which would explain why, when you're under stress, you can make stupid or impulsive decisions. That said, there is now a growing body of research that offers an alternative to MacLean's view of how our brains and emotions work. One proponent of this work is the neuroscientist Dr. Sarah McKay, who emphasizes the importance of rethinking how our so-called reptilian brain operates.

It is now understood that there isn't a hardwired lizard brain "fear" circuit in our brains. The classical triune brain concept implies that all human behavior is driven by fear and that the reptilian brain overpowers our ability to have calm, rational thought. But as Dr. McKay argues, what about the enormous diversity of emotional experiences we are capable of and that deeply move us, such as passionate love, envy, desire, joy, contentment, grief, exhilaration, or tenderness?

Her approach is also supported by Dr. Lisa Feldman Barrett, one of the most cited scientists in the world for her revolutionary research in psychology and neuroscience. She states: "Humans are not at the mercy of mythical emotion circuits buried deep in the animalistic parts of your highly evolved brain: you are architects of your own experience."

What follows is an overview of current thinking on how our brains and bodies process information and in turn how we experience emotions. As you read through this section, consider how these processes might impact you when engaged in any form of negotiation.

What are emotions?

Emotions are made up of many ingredients, including your bodily sensations, your life experiences and expectations, the people you're with, the situation you're in. What ingredients have helped shape the emotion you're feeling at the moment?

Just as you are the architect of your thinking and behavior, you are also the architect of your emotions.

Your emotions are not independent reactions to the world. You are not a passive receiver of sensory input, but rather an active constructor of your emotions. From sensory input and past experience, your brain constructs meaning and prescribes action.

Emotional regulation

You can practice managing your emotions in advance of a stressful event by teaching your brain the most useful way to respond in a situation. Actors do this all the time. The emotions actors show on stage are often real because they rehearsed them.

Worry, for example, is repeating a thought over and over again. You are practicing that thought, and with practice it gets easier to experience over time. You can practice positive thoughts and emotions instead. We all get to choose in any given moment what we focus on, interpret what it means, and then, as a result of that, decide what we are going to do.

Just like a painter learns to see fine distinctions in colors or a wine connoisseur develops their palate to experience tastes non-experts can't distinguish, you can practice naming emotions. With practice, you can become an expert at recognizing and regulating emotions.

Fear and autonomic responses

Another way to help you regulate your emotions is to attempt to identify their individual ingredients, especially your bodily sensations. For example, a fast-beating heart doesn't necessarily mean your brain has detected a threat or there is something to fear. Perhaps your heart is beating faster because you're excited or you're getting ready to exercise?

If someone is scared of a spider, you could ask them to describe the spider using as many emotion words as possible. They might then say, "The spider in front of me makes me feel disgusted, nervous, and jittery but is also kind of intriguing." While the fight-or-flight reflex has helped us survive throughout evolution, most of us rarely find ourselves facing imminent mortal danger these days. That said, modern life still presents situations where you feel threatened, thereby generating an almost impulsive, subconscious decision-making process. These "threats" could include a delay to your train journey, for example.

Your ability to use more of your cortex, rather than allowing the impulsive part of your brain to take over, will enable your responses to be more logical, rational, and objective. It also offers you an opportunity to develop yet another of your superpowers . . .

Patience

Patience helps you to slow everything down, providing you with invaluable breathing space to think objectively and rationally, thereby improving your ability to negotiate effectively. In a tense kidnap negotiation, where the bad guys haven't phoned in weeks and the fear felt by the families and colleagues of the hostage is rising every day, being able to stay calm at the center of the storm is essential. Even more so when everyone's fight-or-flight reflexes are already triggered. This is why it's crucial to develop the ability to withstand uncertainty and be comfortable with being uncomfortable.

After a significant period of such silence, and no doubt under pressure from the family or other key stakeholders, clients often tell me that they want to "review the negotiation strategy." Through experience, I realize that, actually, this is them thinking, "We don't think this is progressing as quickly as we think it should—even though we have zero experience of such negotiations, apart from what we've seen in movies—which is making us feel uncomfortable. We want to replace that feeling with a far more comfortable one, the illusion of control, which really means we want to offer more ransom money."

Each time I hear a variation of this, I acknowledge and align with the client. After all, there's no benefit in me telling them that they're wrong, as this will only encourage them to resist the agreed strategy even more. Then, I empathize with them by saying, "I know this may be painful and frustrating for you to sit through while you wait for the kidnappers to call.

With every passing hour, it must seem like your loved ones are being placed in even more danger and that offering more money now might encourage the kidnappers to release them. This is understandable."

Once I've demonstrated that I've heard and understood what they are saying and feeling, only then can I urge patience and to resist offering more money, as in reality offering more without a reduction in demand would only make the kidnappers believe there is more money available and would likely delay the release of the hostages even more.

Patience is a superpower because it gives you the ability to pause, reflect, and then respond, rather than react as per your habitual (and often detrimental) patterns. It develops clarity of thought, which enables you to bring laser focus to the problem rather than the symptoms. This then gives you the opportunity to come up with an effective solution to any challenge in your daily life, not just in a kidnap negotiation. Like all skills, though, it requires practice, which can be done by simply taking a few seconds to gather your thoughts and take stock of your options when faced with a challenge, from a clear-headed perspective, rather than a knee-jerk reaction.

How Involuntary Urges Conflict with Good Communication

You arrange to meet your partner for dinner, but they're ten minutes late and they're not answering your calls or messages.

- How do you feel?

- What emotions are showing up inside of you?

- Do you feel annoyed or anxious?

Maybe you're telling yourself, "Typical! They're probably having an affair and messaging their lover and lost all track of time!" Or do you stay composed and remain optimistic, thinking, "They're probably

(Continued)

stuck in traffic and their phone is in their bag, which they can't access as they're driving."

Then, when you're faced with intense emotions, such as someone shouting at you, do you simply freeze, not knowing what to say, because your senses are being overwhelmed? Conversely, I'm sure you know people who instinctively fly off the handle and say something inappropriate that they'll later regret.

You may be having an argument with your partner where both of your nervous systems have been hijacked by innate evolutionary processes. For anyone who's ever been in such a situation, you'll know just how impossible it is to have a free-flowing, nonjudgmental, empathetic conversation. Even though you know that your partner is not the enemy, both sides are trying to prove themselves right and the other person wrong. For many of us, we don't even know when that response has been triggered in ourselves, let alone in our partner. So, you continue trying to negotiate, with little success.

Right brain versus left brain

There is another common misconception that the right and left sides of the brain are responsible for completely different things. We equate the left side with analytical thinking and the right side with emotion and creativity. We also believe that all of us tend to favor one side more than the other. However, there is now significant research suggesting that this not the case at all. In fact, both sides of the brain are equally responsible for both rational thinking and emotion. When you understand which cells in which part of the brain manifest particular abilities, the more power you have to choose who and how you want to be in any given moment.

The Harvard-educated neuroanatomist Dr. Jill Bolte Taylor describes in her book *Whole Brain Living* how you have four different "characters" inside your brain and the better you know these characters, the easier your life will become (figure 3-1). The insights came from her experience of suffering a massive stroke on the left side of her brain, which she has also spoken

FIGURE 3-1

Four characters

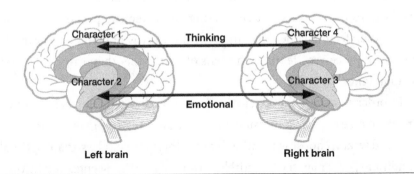

about in her popular TED talk, "My Stroke of Insight," which has been viewed over 28 million times.

Bolte Taylor describes these characters as follows:

Character One (Left-Brain Thinking): If you want to be more productive, then you will want to get to know, respect, and nurture your Left Thinking group of cells. This rational character in your brain is amazingly gifted at creating order in the external world. It's in charge of the to-do list and can be very goal driven. It's also the part of your brain that can be judgmental in defining what is right or wrong, good or bad, based on its moral compass. It is also this character that triggers your stress response, since it is a perfectionist in all it does. This part of your brain cares that the stapler goes back where it belongs and it insists that you color inside the lines. Dr. Bolte Taylor goes on to suggest people name their characters. And for this one, she suggests choosing a name that rings true for your methodical self.

Your relationship to time can also be found in this area. It can be said that time is made up of one chaotic moment after another, so if your Character One is underdeveloped and not encouraged to keep your life orderly, then in no time at all you might shift into your Left-Brain Emotional Character Two and feel overwhelmed, anxious, or hopelessly behind.

Character Two (Left-Brain Emotional): This character likes to protect you from getting hurt and tends to fear the unknown, which is often powered by a familiar feeling of unease that stems from trauma or something unresolved from your past. As a result, this Character Two part of your brain may end up feeling either "less than" or not worthy of being loved, simply because it perceives life through a lens of lack, rather than through a filter of abundance.

In order to escape these negative emotions or disappointments, which are based on external circumstances, your Character Two may become anxious and weary, choosing to either blame others for your less-than-optimal conditions, or it may try to entirely escape your pain by engaging in your favorite form of distraction, such as binge-watching Netflix when you know you should be preparing for that important presentation. The name given to this part of your brain, according to Bolte Taylor, should sum up your deepest fear or emotional wound. Knowing this part of yourself and learning how you can self-soothe your own little Character Two by using your other characters is key to feeling okay again after you have been emotionally triggered.

Learning how to identify and embody all four of your characters, and then choosing to step into the strong, compassionate, and loving parts of yourself when you need to, has the power to lift us out of our Character Two's tantrums, discomfort, and pain. It is so important for your individual personal growth, as well as how you show up in your communication with others, that you wade into and reflect on your Character Two pain. But it is equally critical that you only visit there and don't adopt it as a lifestyle. We are about to find out, however, that your right brain, Characters Three and Four, is all about the present moment.

Character Three (Right-Brain Emotional): This is your emotional, experiential self, who seeks similarities rather than differences with other people out of a desire to connect, explore, and go on adventures with others. The way the present moment *feels* can be insightful and fun, as well as deeply connecting through empathy. This is also the character that might struggle with "shiny object syndrome," always moving toward the next fun or interesting thing.

When considering a name for this character, you might want to choose one that invokes curiosity *and* chaos. As life can be seen as being composed of consecutive moments of disarray, most of which are outside of your control, this part of you is where you get to play and be creative, singing at the top of your lungs, creating art with abandon, and exploring nature without a schedule.

Character Four (Right-Brain Thinking): This is the Right Thinking part of your brain, which exists as your most peaceful, open-hearted, and generous loving self. Character Four is completely invested in celebrating the gift of life with immense openness, gratitude, and acceptance. When you meditate, pray, or repeat a positive affirmation or self-talk, for example, you are quietening your left-brain Characters One and Two, so you can experience the calmness of your Character Four. It is always there and available for you to tune in to. The type of name to choose for this character wants to invoke something grand and interconnected, a name that enables you to gain easy access to this innermost part of who you are.

To summarize, consider your left side as being driven by "me," firmly caught between the regret of your past and your anxieties of the future. The right side, meanwhile, is where "me" becomes "we," enabling you to appreciate that life consists only of present moments. You need to get all four characters working together, with the shared goal of maximizing your well-being and making good decisions, especially when you're under stress and more likely to make bad choices.

When something triggers you, you have ninety seconds when the chemicals associated with an emotion flood your body, after which you can choose to either keep feeding that emotion or select another, more helpful approach. Ignoring your feelings is not an option. The feeling part of your brain is far more dominant than the thinking part. As Bolte Taylor reminds us: "We are feeling creatures who think, rather than thinking creatures who feel." So, take the time to get to know your four characters, and identify the ones currently dominating your life.

Consider utilizing the following five-part process, which Bolte Taylor calls "the BRAIN huddle," to bring together your four characters to decide which one you want to embody in any given moment, which in turn can help you make the better decisions:

1. **Breathe:** Connect with your breathing.

2. **Recognize:** Which of the four characters are you currently in?

3. **Appreciate:** Acknowledge and appreciate the character you've identified.

4. **Inquire:** Which character is most appropriate to handle this situation?

5. **Navigate:** Recognize the power of change and the fact that you have the ability to choose which character you want to bring forward in the next moment.

Finally, remember, you have the power to choose who and how you want to be in any given moment, so give your four characters names that honor their identities and you will end up truly mastering your emotions.

But what happens when you fail to deal with the natural fight, flight, or freeze impulses appropriately? What are the negative impacts of stress on your body and mind? What happens when you're faced with either a tsunami of adversity or maybe a stream of "microaggressions"?

Think about how you respond to subtle yet hostile verbal and behavioral slights, all stacking up waiting for the proverbial straw to break the camel's back.

The negative impacts of stress

If you ever need another reminder of why being able to control the impact of stress on your body by developing a well-trained, resilient mindset is the key to negotiating effectively over the long term, then consider the following chemical and structural changes that occur in every system in your body if you don't deal with stress:

Nervous system: Development of tumors, cerebral hemorrhages, aneurysms, strokes, dementia, cognitive impairment, depression, memory loss

Circulatory system: Constricts arterial system, promotes cardio-vascular disease, and causes changes in blood pressure and heart rate

Endocrine system: Release of cortisol and ACTH (adrenocortico-tropic) hormone, which stimulates the adrenal cortex and leads to compromised adrenal glands, thyroid malfunction, weight gain; can cause diabetes, decreased immune cell count, and eventually cancer

Digestive system: Nervous stomach, nausea, bleeding ulcers, spastic colon, ulcerative colitis

The psychological impacts of stress, meanwhile, include reduced productivity, impaired judgment, increased mental confusion, compromised restorative sleep, and can lead to addictions (drugs, alcohol, food, nicotine, sugar, caffeine).

Stress-busting techniques to gain laser focus and clarity

If there is a certain inevitability about how your body is triggered during stressful situations, what can you do to mitigate it? The secret lies in an understanding of your autonomic nervous system (ANS). Classified by the British physiologist John Langley in the early 1900s, the ANS connects your central nervous system with almost all of your internal organs. As a result, it is responsible for controlling basic life functions such as blood circulation, digestion, respiration, and temperature regulation. It is so powerful; it keeps us alive without us having to physically think or do anything to make it work.

Langley divided the autonomic system into two. The parasympathetic system is responsible for resting, digesting, and recovery, while the sympathetic system, which manages your fight, flight, or freeze response, keeps your innate immunity machine working effectively. Only one system can be dominant at any one time, which is why it's important that you balance your ANS in order to realize its benefits of developing a resilient mindset and living a balanced and healthy life.

Modern life often prevents us from achieving this balance, and you usually spend more time with your sympathetic system running the show. When you focus or linger on your stress for too long, your sympathetic system continuously releases cortisol, and the resulting chronic elevated levels can lead to serious issues. These include prolonged stress, which sends the sympathetic response into overdrive, resulting in chronic inflammation and illness. That's why sufficient time needs to be spent with the parasympathetic system at the wheel in order to counterbalance the harm caused by its opposite.

The following are some effective and proven methods to reduce your stress response in real time, as well as techniques for long-term stress management to bring the two systems back into balance. Using these methods has enabled me to become a far more effective negotiator.

How do you cope when triggered?

Maybe you reach for your mobile phone, cigarettes, or junk food. Or, do you exercise, journal, or meditate? Each time you feel a trigger, you get to choose in that very moment which response will truly serve you. If you get it right, you can utilize the gap, however short, between the trigger and what you do next and commit to responding in a positive way. This allows you to gracefully move through life, as Victor Frankl suggested, by responding rather than merely reacting to events, which are often outside your immediate control, in any event.

By doing so, you can live with authenticity and meaning, and move through life always able to become the calm at the center of any storm raging around you. By exposure to and overcoming stress, you can also train yourself to stay centered, present, and in control so you can balance competing demands, boost your mood and energy to improve your relationships, and improve your life.

What can you do about it?

At any given time, one or more of the following things are going on inside you:

- Thinking thoughts

- Feeling emotions

- Having a physiological response to those thoughts and to what you're thinking and feeling

For example, if you're having a thought that is resulting in a physiological response, such as anger, then the chemical noradrenaline is pumped into your bloodstream. From the first moment the thought arises until the noradrenaline is flushed completely out of your bloodstream takes less than ninety seconds. Now, I know lots of people, myself included, who have stayed angry for a whole lot longer than ninety seconds. This is because you keep running the same story on loop over and over!

The key is to stay focused on your body. Ask yourself: Is your heart beating fast? Is there a churning sensation in your stomach? A tightness across your chest or shoulders? Feel the feeling and then drop the story that you are associating with causing this particular emotion. The overwhelming urge to justify or to assign blame for why you're feeling it is simply a defense mechanism designed to prevent you from being uncomfortable. Yet within the discomfort lies the solution. By giving it space to flow through you, it will dissipate and provide you with a calmness from which to then think about your situation more objectively and rationally than you might have done otherwise.

• • •

The following negotiation case file demonstrates this in action.

Negotiation Case File #4: Middle East

I'm sitting at a long wooden table in a windowless room, thousands of miles from home. I can hear the low rumble of the creaking air-conditioning unit that provides background accompaniment to the tension lying thick in the air. A stale and decaying odor lingers around my nostrils. In front of me on the table is an old Nokia mobile phone. All eyes in the room are staring at it, willing it to ring.

My job here as the response consultant is to be the trusted adviser to those in the room, who comprise company middle management as well as senior government and other agency officials. The phone hasn't rung in weeks, and I'm fighting the urge to question the strategy I so confidently recommended to the CMT now sitting nervously around me.

I stand up and walk over to the other side of the room and pour myself a coffee. In walks a man-mountain of a guy, whom I'll call John. He reaches out and shakes my hand; his feels like steel in a velvet glove. He has a crooked, yet warm smile and asks me, not for the first time, "Mr. Scott, why do the kidnappers not call?"

"We must be patient. They will call when they are good and ready," I reply.

I am using John to communicate with the kidnappers primarily due to language and dialect. Also, if I jump on the calls and begin negotiating myself, this will only increase the perceived value of the six hostages in the eyes of the kidnappers. I can't allow that to happen, because the kidnappers will then, wrongly, believe they'll be able to get more money, which will, in turn, increase the risk to the hostages' lives.

As we both sit back down at the table, the shrill ringtone of the phone makes the others in the room jump. More than one of them stifles a nervous laugh, releasing the tension slightly. John looks at me and I nod as he presses the green "Accept" button.

"Hello!" shouts an unfamiliar and aggressive voice with a heavy accent.

"Yes, hello, my friend. We are here to help," replies John politely.

"We have your people. We want $3 million or else they die. No excuses, no police. We'll call back." The call is abruptly ended.

All eyes in the room shift from the phone to me, as they search for certainty in a scenario that has this in short supply. And so, the games begin.

The days roll by quickly as John initially does a great job, exuding calm and a willingness to follow my guidance on what to say and when to say it. We rehearse the scripts and practice worst-case scenarios of answering and responding to the most difficult questions the kidnappers could ask us, not to mention dealing with the death threats and mock executions we're likely to receive.

Over the next couple of weeks, the negotiations move back and forth, with us offering what is referred to in the industry as "decreasing increases." This involves offering less and less money each time as the negotiations progress. Of course, it's all dependent on the kidnappers playing their part by significantly reducing their demands each time too. Which they do; we get them down to $400,000.

This isn't primarily about trying to save money, even though in reality the client doesn't have anywhere near $3 million (and the kidnappers know that by now). This is about paying an appropriate amount in the shortest period of time, while militating against any future kidnappings. If we pay too much, too quickly, then the kidnappers will think, "This is easy" and could take the money but not release the hostages, a technique called "doubling." The way to avoid this scenario is to maintain negotiation discipline and emotional regulation throughout. Or, they'll agree to release the hostages and then just kidnap them or a colleague or family member again the following week.

Our success is short-lived, however, as things are about to take a turn for the worse. The pressure of being the primary communicator is finally getting to John. He hasn't shaved in days or showered in longer. I know this because I've sat next to him for sixteen hours every day for almost a month. He's a broken man.

We have managed to build rapport with the kidnappers, and we're now in a good place with one another. The finish line is almost in sight. My concern is that if John doesn't have the right mindset and stay calm at the center of this storm, it will create significant challenges in the negotiation. Any unnecessary delay only puts the lives of the hostages in even greater danger. Especially as we're about to enter one of the most challenging and fraught phases of the entire negotiation.

All eyes are now on me, both in-country and back at headquarters in London, to get a grip on this and get things moving. My experience tells me I can afford to leave the kidnappers stewing for a couple of days, as they aren't going anywhere. I have to focus all my attention on John and help him get in the right state to manage his emotions. If not, we could have six dead hostages and I'd be looking for a career change.

My thoughts are interrupted by the now-familiar shrill ringtone of the old mobile phone, vibrating on the table.

"Hello. We are here," John answers, without looking up. The tiredness evident in his voice.

"Do you have our money?" demands the now-familiar, but still un-known, voice on the other end.

"My friend, you must understand, we are a poor company and the amount you ask for is simply too much. And please, look after my people; they are your responsibility," John pleads.

"No! They are yours. Pay the money by Friday or you'll never see them again." The call ends abruptly once again.

Silence hangs in the air. No one moves. That is until John's huge fist comes slamming down hard on the wooden table. In that moment, I in-voluntarily move back, as I realize it's about to come my way too.

John stands and shouts in my direction, "How can you sit there all calm, when my friends are about to die?"

There is no point in attempting to rationalize with him, as his brain won't hear the words due to the high levels of anxiety he is experiencing. He pauses, turns away, and then storms out of the room.

This is not a good moment. I need to help him. Fast.

John is the key to this negotiation working. Without him being in a great state, harnessing all of the innate power from his very own Red Center and actually seeing and believing this working out for the best, we are screwed. The kidnappers can wait. We have several hundred thousand dollars on the table in real cash, ready to be bagged up and handed over. They know they're not going to get more. They just want to save face and squeeze every last drop from us. But I'm going to get them to work for it. I reckon we have a couple of days in which we can turn the phone off and ignore the kidnap-pers, and for me to turn John around.

Before I do though, I must first check in with my own state and mindset, as this will inevitably impact John's, as we saw earlier with Betari's Box. I also need to balance compassion with the courage not to "sugarcoat the grenade"; I must say what needs to be said to him clearly and directly.

I follow him outside into the courtyard and stand directly in front of him, firmly grounded, tapping into my own Red Center, certain in my intent. The first thing I must do is validate his emotions and reassure him that it's perfectly understandable for him to take it personally that six of his colleagues have been kidnapped at gunpoint on his watch. Right now, he just needs his worldview to be seen, heard, and understood. That said, it's also futile to play the blame game, as it only disengages and dilutes a person's problem-solving capabilities, usually followed by other destructive emotions, such as resentment and hatred.

We spend the rest of the day and the following morning just the two of us, walking around the compound, spending time balancing out his nervous system, reducing the anxiety and increasing the calm, rational, objective, thinking behavior most needed to help us succeed.

As we'll cover in more detail later in the book, John is not going to be able to make this work until he regains his trust in me and feels psychologically safe and cared for in my presence. He needs to feel seen, heard, and understood.

We also spend time helping him to tune in to what he is feeling in his body. Where is the tension and the frustration showing up? Once these are located and identified, I take him through some breathing techniques to allow them to dissolve and dissipate.

We then go through the three key steps I know will enable him to re-engage. First, I ask: "What are you focusing on?" All of us have the ability to decide where we place our attention, and John's is currently fixed not only on what has gone wrong but on what could go wrong in the future. Rather than seeing the huge gains and progress we have made in the negotiation, he is catastrophizing. I get him to reframe the situation into one involving hope and to see how well set up we are as a team. We are in the best possible position to resolve this case.

Second, I get him to decide what meaning he wants to give the situation we're in. At the moment, he is making the burden heavier by giving his focus a disempowering meaning—that he is somehow to blame for his colleagues being taken hostage and that he is failing them by not having secured their release by now. Instead, he could accept that we are doing absolutely everything we can to secure their freedom and recognize that the chances of success are high. Or he could honor the hostages by reframing the meaning to one of certainty that we are going to get them out alive and that he is the best person to help with that.

Based on his initial negative focus and disempowering meaning, he took ineffective and unhelpful action by not looking after himself physically and mentally and by not following the tools and techniques I had shown him. By positively reframing the answers to these questions and coming up with empowering alternative answers, it shifts your focus, meaning, and action into momentum you can use to turn those huge boulders you perceive to be blocking your path into tiny pieces of gravel that you can easily kick out of the way.

Thankfully, John reengages, following the negotiation strategy that has been agreed on by all of the CMT, because only by following these steps will we all succeed. The following day, John walks into the conference room showered, shaved, and with the energy of a new man. We switch the kidnappers' phone back on, and within the hour they call. With his renewed mindset and enhanced powers, we negotiate the ransom even lower.

Within another week, we agree a final ransom of $127,000, down from that initial demand of $3 million. Forty-eight hours later, all hostages are released without harm and I'm sitting with them, debriefing them on their experiences.

———— • • • ————

While it is unlikely that you'll find yourself in exactly the same circumstances as this scenario, it is likely that you'll find yourself in your own version of it. You might be having a tough conversation with a member of your team or in your personal life, when negative emotions, thoughts, and behavior impact the quality of the communication. Or you may know someone who is experiencing such a challenge. At this point, asking yourself or the other person the following questions might help:

1. **What am I focusing on right now?** Is it the end of a relationship or a new beginning? Am I focusing on what's not going well or things that I can be grateful for?

2. **What does this mean?** You are a meaning-making machine, and the language you use to interpret and make sense of something will determine the emotion or state you experience in that moment. From the earlier example, your partner is late for your dinner date and hasn't messaged you to tell you the reason. Are you angry and frustrated, or concerned and understanding?

3. **What am I going to do?** Now that you've chosen your focus and given it its meaning, you'll then decide what to do, based on those two other factors. Do you leave the restaurant fuming or manage to take back control of those powerful emotions?

Now you know what's going on inside of the brain and body, you can begin to take back control of those emotions that regularly show up and threaten your balance, setting you up to negotiate with your emotions in check. Remember, when you're hit with a stressful situation, regardless of what it is, allow yourself to observe your surrounding emotions for a full ninety seconds.

How to overcome this evolutionary emotional hijack

As mentioned earlier, when you are triggered and overwhelmed with stress, the amygdala is activated, that part of your two-million-year-old brain designed to warn us about saber-toothed tigers. This is sometimes referred to as the "amygdala hijack." Powerful chemicals, including adrenaline and cortisol, pump through your body for approximately ninety seconds. It is worth noting here that your response to such stress is hardwired, meaning it's very hard to prevent such a response from happening in the first place.

How do you achieve this?

There are several technology-enabled ways to balance these two parts of your ANS and thereby overcome your primitive survival function and manage stress on your terms. One I use on a regular basis, particularly when deployed on a tense kidnapping negotiation, is listening to the NuCalm App for about twenty minutes a day. The app has a variety of audio tracks set at different frequencies, which I find to be a quick way of relaxing and countering the effects of cortisol and adrenaline while increasing levels of focus and concentration. Initially created to treat people with posttraumatic stress disorder, NuCalm is now used by everyone from dental patients suffering from anxiety to some of the top sports teams and business leaders in the world.

However, you're not always going to have headphones and smartphone apps at hand to bring about this balanced state of mind. Thankfully, there are other, more traditional methods to reduce stress that are always available, no matter where you are in the world and whatever the circumstances.

- **Step 1:** Awareness within your body of where you feel the stress; for example, churning in the stomach or tightness across the chest. Then acknowledge that this is happening, rather than denying it.

- **Step 2:** Name it to tame it. Whatever and wherever the feeling is, if you can name the associated emotion, the feeling will gradually reduce.

- **Step 3:** Ride the wave. At this stage you simply have to feel the feeling and drop any associated story as to what may have caused it, as if you're on a surfboard riding the waves for ninety seconds. Doing so will also diminish the sensation.

Harnessing the power of the breath

There is significant research behind the positive effects of various breathing techniques on your nervous system to reduce feelings of stress and increase the experience of calmness.

Physiological sigh

A Stanford University experiment studied the "physiological sigh" pattern of breathing, in which two inhales through the nose are followed by an extended exhale through the mouth.

The double inhale of the physiological sigh "pops" the air sacs (alveoli) in the lungs open, allowing oxygen in and enabling carbon dioxide to be offloaded during the long exhale. The long sigh out encourages the heart rate to slow, mitigating the physical feelings that come along with acute stress. In the exercises below, you'll see how effective breathing techniques are in managing your state and nervous system.

Box breathing

Like the physiological sigh, box breathing also manipulates carbon dioxide levels in the bloodstream to manage stress. However, this technique works by allowing it to build up. By holding your breath, you allow carbon dioxide to build in the blood, which in turn activates the parasympathetic branch of the nervous system, resulting in a sense of calm. Box breathing consists of four stages, of four counts each:

1. Inhale through the nose, while counting to four in your head.

2. Hold your breath for another four counts.

3. Exhale through the mouth for a count of four.

4. Hold your breath for a final four count.

Repeat these two or three times.

Cold therapy

Exposing yourself to some form of cold triggers the release of noradrenaline and dopamine in the brain, promoting a sense of calm alertness. You could take a cold shower (at a safe but uncomfortable temperature) or stand in a cryotherapy chamber to reduce your body temperature. This is thought to build resilience under controlled circumstances, better equipping you to deal with larger stressors in the future.

Sleep

While you might not think that there's the opportunity in the middle of a tense kidnap negotiation to focus on getting decent sleep, imposing a call window with the kidnappers from the outset allows us to have the "nego-tiator phone" switched on for only a short period each day. This enables everyone involved to get some much-needed rest.

Even in everyday negotiations, prioritizing sleep is vital to performing at your very best. Would you expect your mobile phone or laptop to work well, even when they aren't charged every day? How long would you be able to use them before they ran out of juice? You may think this isn't a rele-vant comparison, but what is your mind and body if not a highly tuned supercomputer? Like your devices, it needs recharging and looking after if you want to be able to show up at the negotiation table with the best pos-sible mindset and strategy.

While there may be a requirement for the occasional all-nighter to get a deal over the line, submit a report or assignment, or travel across multiple time zones, focusing on getting decent sleep is imperative to achieving long-term, sustainable success and being able to negotiate effectively.

In fact, chronic sleep deprivation itself acts as a stressor to the body, re-sulting in increased production of cortisol and adrenaline, which puts the sympathetic nervous system into overdrive, ultimately leading to burnout, or worse.

Mindfulness

This much-misunderstood technique is a top-down method of addressing stress. It can be used to build resilience in stressful moments, as well as to alleviate symptoms of stress in real time. You don't have to sit on the floor and chant or try to empty your mind, as popular culture might have you believe. Mindfulness is simply focused awareness. You can begin by sitting or lying in a comfortable position and noticing how your body is experi-encing stress. Feel the feeling while dropping the story or reasoning about why. You might say instead: "My stomach is churning" or "My shoulders feel tight."

Movement

Exercise reduces levels of adrenaline and cortisol while promoting endorphin production. And, in the long term, it protects the body from the harmful effects of chronic stress and inflammation while priming your adaptation to the stress response. Doing between 120 and 200 minutes of exercise (at the intensity where you can hold a conversation) per week has been proven to prevent all-cause mortality by 50 percent. This is why, when deployed on a kidnap case, taking time out of the day to exercise is actively encouraged for everyone in the CMT.

Now that you know what's happening inside you and the other person you're communicating with, it's time to look at some techniques that will help us negotiate better.

Technique 9: Proactive Listening, Establishing Rapport, Trust-Based Influence

We know that words matter. But not, it would seem, if you fall for one of the most common communication myths out there. The one that states our body language accounts for 55 percent of our communication, whereas our tone accounts for 38 percent and only 7 percent for the actual words we use. In the study on which these figures are based, which was conducted in 1967 by the scientists Albert Mehrabian and Morton Wiener, participants were read a list of words (such as *dear, honey, really,* and *brute*) in either a neutral, negative, or positive tone and shown photos of either matching or inconsistent facial expressions. It is worth noting that these images only showed facial expressions and no other part of the body.

Given the limitations in the experiment's methodology, it should come as no surprise that the total nonverbal element of both tone (38 percent) and body language (55 percent) scored as high as 93 percent.

Years later, Mehrabian sought to clarify the misinterpretation by explaining the study was about looking for inconsistencies between the words a person is saying and their nonverbal behavior. If there is any discrepancy, then emphasis should be on "listening" to the nonverbal cues. When we look for them, such inconsistencies are commonplace in both the home and workplace. In summary, what you say is less important than how you say it. That said, all three elements of communication are vitally important and allow us to develop a more accurate understanding of the other person.

Listening is hard work. I don't mean the sort of listening you do when you're on the phone while watching the TV on mute in the background. Or when a client is talking to you in a meeting or on a video call and you find yourself thinking about what you need to pick up on your way home from the shops. I'm talking here about real listening that requires every fiber of your being to remain present and actively engaged.

Being able to master the skill of active listening is fundamental if you want to collaborate with, influence, and persuade people anywhere, anytime, on anything. Maybe you get triggered when you're unfairly criticized, or perhaps you have a client who for some reason you simply can't seem to connect with as well as others. What does this mean? It's likely you're focusing on you rather than the other person. And remember: *it's not about you.*

When you are spoken to like this, imagine that you don't allow yourself to be triggered and you're able to hear where this person is coming from and help them meet their needs. You can do this because you've made the issue the adversary and not the person. Picture that same client saying: "It feels like you really understand the challenges we're facing, almost like you're able to read my mind."

So, are you ready to learn how to master this number-one skill used by hostage negotiators the world over to bring about behavioral change in another person, regardless of background, culture, circumstances, education, or language?

I believe you'll get there by taking Ernest Hemingway's advice: "When people talk, listen completely. Most people never listen." If you do so, you'll learn *the* most powerful Jedi-mind trick of them all—level-five listening. Have you ever experienced a time when someone has made you feel truly seen, heard, and understood? Chances are, they were using level-five listening. How amazing would it be if all your clients or the people you negotiate with felt that way too?

The five levels of listening

As you go through the levels that follow, think about how often you spend at each level. The first three levels are when the focus is all on you, rather than the person you're communicating with.

Level one: Listening for gist

The first level of listening can be seen as intermittent listening. Here, you're simply listening for long enough to get the gist of what the other side is saying. When you've got the basic idea, your ears shut off and you refocus on your internal voice, which is formulating a reaction based on your world-view. Though you might not articulate this reaction, you're engaged in an internal dialogue about how what is being said doesn't line up with your logic. This is also the "rabbit caught in the headlights moment," when you're asked a question when you haven't been listening.

Another example is when one person might be watching television or scrolling through social media while having a conversation with someone. An example of this might occur when you're on a video call, but are thinking about an Amazon delivery you're expecting or maybe drafting an email at the same time as the other person is talking.

Level two: Listening to rebut

At this next level, you're not practicing active listening at all. You're simply pretending to listen so you can rebut. This is the stage at which you listen for long enough to understand the incoming message until it hits the trigger (i.e., something in the statement or phrase that you can argue against or rebut). When you hear it, you just wait for the other side to shut up for long enough so you can tell them why their position is faulty and, by extension, how much smarter you are than them. These enthusiastic replies undermine communication and the entire relationship. Often, interjecting with a quick response is a clear indication that you are not listening. How could you be? At this level, you're focusing on your agenda at the expense of theirs and it's obvious.

Listening at this level also occurs when people talk over one another, with neither side really feeling like they're being heard. You may also find yourself at this level if you're waiting to talk and working out what you're going to say while the other person is still talking, rather than truly engaging with what they are saying.

Level three: Listening for logic

This third level involves using inference to try to pin down the internal logic of what the other person is saying, if indeed such logic exists. Is this their worldview on a particular topic, such as climate change, for example? How have they come to their conclusion or judgment? Why is their viewpoint important to them? This is not a case of asking them a lot of questions to elicit this information. If we listen deeply enough, the logic behind their position will usually become apparent. This is the first step toward truly understanding the person you're negotiating with.

At the next two levels, the focus shifts to *them*.

Level four: Listening for emotion

At the fourth level, you're listening for any emotions or issues that may be driving their argument. It's irrelevant whether these emotions or issues make sense to you. At this level, you recognize their significance as they talk about what's important to them. When it's your turn to respond, you might decide to use a form of labeling, such as, "It sounds like you're frustrated with our counteroffer." This identifies the unstated emotions you believe are influencing what they have to say.

Another example is if your counterpart gives you an energetic response to your statement, you might say something like, "It seems like you're very passionate about this deal," in the hope they will reveal additional information. We will cover labeling and other active listening techniques in more detail later in the book.

This level also involves tuning in to try to uncover the primary emotions that might be behind what the other person is saying, including reflecting the emotions back to them. It also begins to provide you with some clarity about their model of the world and how they view life, what motivates or scares them. You will be reflecting back to them what you're hearing and understanding of what they're saying.

Level five: Listening for point of view

This is where you become a world-class communicator. It's the level where you listen to the other side's argument to interpret who they perceive themselves to be in the world, using an empathetic curiosity to see things from their perspective. Using this type of curiosity is how you filter their emotion and logic to get a deeper understanding of them. How can you expect to influence or persuade someone, let alone close that all-important deal, if you don't first seek to understand where they're coming from? Make no mistake, this level of listening is hard work. Which is why you need to practice it as often as you can, so when the opportunity presents itself, you'll be ready, willing, and able to succeed.

Listening at this level requires a depth of curiosity that cannot be forced, and it can only take place when you are in a state of flow. If you recall, it was Kotler who said a state of flow is when "you are so focused on the task at hand that everything else falls away. Action and awareness merge. Time flies. The Self vanishes. Performance goes through the roof."

In a state of flow, this kind of listening should feel effortless, as your sensory acuity will be heightened, picking up the space in between the speaker's words and discerning their real needs and what drives them. At levels Four and Five, you're able to ask questions that promote discovery and insight for the other person, and maybe challenge some of their old assumptions or "stories." And as a result, you've earned their trust and can begin to influence and ultimately achieve cooperation and even behavior change.

When have you caught yourself (or been caught) in levels One, Two, or Three? When have you been in levels Four or Five? How did it feel?

What is active listening?

In addition to building rapport, gaining trust, and influencing behavior, it's important to remember that your voice may be your strongest tool. You rarely remember the words somebody used, but you sure as hell remember their tone of voice and how they made you feel.

In 1957, the American psychologist Carl Rogers and his colleague Richard Farson coined the term "active listening," in a book of the same name, as something that "requires that we get inside the speaker, that we grasp, from his point of view, just what it is he is communicating to us. More than that, we must convey to the speaker that we are seeing things from his point of view."

Rogers devised this system of active listening, which encouraged a person to discuss what is on their minds. The beauty of active listening is that its application is universal, as it can be used everywhere from a hostage negotiation and therapy to the boardroom and in the home. It also requires practice and effort and is ideal for those moments when something more is at stake.

Active listening is about fully listening to the person before you respond. When you practice active listening, you will hear the justification for their actions, which in turn will enable you to understand their values and beliefs. It demonstrates empathy, builds rapport, and will give you a fuller picture of the route to a safe communication outcome, helping you to problem solve. Keep the conversation centered on their agenda and do not ask too many questions. Listen to their fears and help the person save face. This builds trust, which is the key to effective communication. The more a person talks, the more they will disclose.

Active Listening Myth-Buster

There is a myth about active listening. Almost every book out there on effective communication or negotiation portrays active listening or some of its components as the "gold dust" or "secret sauce" to succeed every time. While active listening is absolutely fundamental to being able to win any negotiation and to influencing and persuading other people, rather than viewing it in isolation, it should be seen as a key part of a much wider negotiator's toolkit, which we'll cover in this section.

MOREPIES is a useful mnemonic to remember the various active listening techniques you have in your communication toolkit as a level-five listener.

Minimal encouragers

Using minimal encouragers such as "and?," "really?," "then?," "mmm," "uh-huh," "go on," "great," and "interesting" are important, particularly during telephone conversations, as people need to know that you are listening, even more so when one person has been speaking for an extended period. By showing that you are paying attention, you encourage the other person to keep talking, feel understood, and thereby build rapport.

Minimal encouragers can be used in every conversation. Ensure you're in alignment when you are using them, though. If you misplace an "encourager" because you're distracted, you'll damage your credibility and shut down the conversation. Finally, match the pace of your "encouragers" to the other person's speed of talking, slowly changing the pace to suit your preference, and be careful of overusing the word "okay," as it can act as a full stop, indicating that you understand or agree.

Open questions

Open questions encourage people to speak freely and to share their side of the story. In a similar way to minimal encouragers, these types of questions encourage the other person in a conversation to continue talking with more than just a "yes" or "no" answer. In any negotiation, particularly in business, the more the other side is communicating with you, the better, because they reveal more of their hand the more they speak. You will discover what's important (and not so important) to them, their pain points, the so-called "red lines" they can't or won't cross, areas where an agreement may be possible, and much more. In a crisis negotiation, where a person may be in distress and considering either suicide or hurting someone else, all the time they're talking they're refraining from doing so.

On the one hand, open questions provide more time to gather information and clear up misunderstandings. They're also good for defusing emotions because they can encourage the other person to think logically and, if they're thinking in this way, it reduces any heightened emotion.

Closed questions, on the other hand, are often seen as the poor cousin to the open variety, yet both types are important and have their place in effective communication. Closed questions are particularly helpful when we need to find out specific information. For example, if someone is talking about self-harming themselves with a knife, I might ask them, "Do you have a knife with you now?" or "Are you having thoughts of doing this now?" as these will likely elicit a "yes" or "no" response. But too many closed questions can sound like an interrogation.

Powerful, open questions usually start with "What" or "How," such as:

- What is our outcome here?

- How will we know this has been a success?

- What is the real issue?

- What is likely to get in the way of...?

- What has to happen in order for...?

- How will this impact...?

- What other options do you have?

Asking "why" questions can sound accusatory or judgmental, and they are therefore unhelpful in a negotiation. An easy way of asking "why" is to replace this word with "what." For example, rather than asking your teenage daughter, "Why on earth do you want to go to that party?" You could ask, "What is it about this party that makes you want to go to it?"

So, by replacing "why" with "what" or even "how" questions, you'll encourage the other person to do the "heavy lifting" and nudge them to come up with possible solutions to the problem. They can also help you say no without using the word "no."

Finally, once you've asked your question, remain quiet to allow a response. Many people follow up on an open question by asking a closed question, which demonstrates that you are not interested in their answer to your first question or you believe you already know the answer.

Reflecting or mirroring

Reflecting back or mirroring the last one to three words or key phrases from the other person's statement is nonconfrontational and demonstrates you have heard them. This technique can be particularly useful in the stages of a conversation when you're seeking to obtain information and build rapport. It also works well during a stressful conversation as it can help orient a conversation and buy you time if you're unsure about how to respond to what is being said. Conversely, "reflecting" or "mirroring" allows you to direct the conversation by choosing which words to reflect back. Be flexible in the words you choose. If your choice does not steer the conversation in the direction you want, pick another.

An example of this technique in the workplace between you and a member of your team might look like:

> *Boss:* "I've noticed a drop in your sales performance over the last couple of weeks and wanted to make sure everything was okay."

> *Employee:* "Yeah. It's just been a struggle following the new procedures, that's all."

> *Boss:* "New procedures?"

In this example, if you use an upward intonation on the "reflection" or "mirror," you're signaling to the other person to continue and expand on what they're saying. If you use a more neutral or downward tone, it will convey a desire to close or end that aspect of the dialogue.

A word of caution here. Out of all the techniques available to you within the MOREPIES framework, reflecting/mirroring and minimal encouragers are the most likely to create a misalignment. This is because the other person may misinterpret your repetition of their words as a challenge or somehow calling into question what they've said, particularly if using an upward intonation, leading to a very awkward "Why are you repeating what I say?" comment. Nevertheless, this technique can be very powerful if used wisely and sparingly and should still form part of every world-class communicator's toolkit.

Emotional labeling (name it to tame it)

Emotions can easily cause a person's behavior to move away from objective and rational thinking as they sense they are losing control. We'll cover how to have meaningful yet difficult and emotional conversations with people later in this book. For now, an overview of the emotional labeling technique will provide you with a highly effective means of developing that all-important rapport.

Emotional labeling allows you to provide a verbal observation of how you think the person you're communicating with is feeling and the problems they're facing. We call this "name it to tame it." Once we've identified either the presenting or underlying emotion, we can begin to tame and manage it. This approach enables you to express your opinion in a non-judgmental way that does not offend and allows them the opportunity to agree or disagree with you. Either way, you will find out what the other person is feeling. This technique extends beyond just emotions and can also be used to label behavior and body language.

Use this technique to gain clarity about what you think people are saying or feeling and what is important to them. Avoid *telling* the other person how they feel and use phrases such as:

"*You sound* annoyed with me."

"*I hear that* the money is important to you."

"*It appears that* . . ."

"*I sense you* . . ."

"*It seems like* you're frustrated with . . ."

"*I get the impression* that . . ."

Rest assured, it doesn't matter if you label their emotion or behavior incorrectly, as long as you haven't rushed in to assume it without spending time to make sure it's evident. The fact that you're making the effort to develop a deeper understanding by acknowledging what is going on for them will likely override any labeling mistake.

While questioning or commenting on the validity of their emotions at this stage is not part of this technique, validation statements, such as, "It's understandable to feel angry that . . ." can be helpful to incorporate into a sensitive or difficult conversation.

Every time you sense that their emotions, behavior, or body language has shifted is an opportunity to offer another label. Applying this to their positive emotions and behavior seeks to reinforce and encourage them further, whereas labeling, rather than dismissing, negative emotions will dilute them.

Examples of labels to use to help you identify emotions or reasons that are causing certain behaviors:

It looks like . . . (fill in the perceived emotion or behavior here)

It sounds like . . .

It seems like . . .

Paraphrasing

This technique involves putting your understanding of what the other person said into *your* words, rather than theirs, and offering this back to them. This time, it's about focusing on the content rather than the emotions, as well as not trying to remember and use their exact words, which is "summarizing" and is the next technique we'll discuss.

What paraphrasing does is allow the other person to clarify or amend if they feel you haven't quite understood what they meant. Clarity is crucial in all forms of communication, but particularly so in high-stakes negotiation. In a kidnapping, paraphrasing would always be used in response to ransom demands to ensure that there are no misunderstandings.

Some ways of starting a paraphrase can include:

"What you're saying is...?"

"Can I share with you where I think you're at with this?"

"What I'm hearing here is... Is that correct?"

Paraphrasing is helpful if you feel the need to get a sense of where you think the other person is at and to check in that you've understood them. This will be one of those rare times that it's okay to interrupt someone talking, particularly if they're communicating a lengthy piece of information. It can also be used if you just need to stall for time or if you're unsure about where to take the conversation next.

"I" statements

In any difficult conversation you will inevitably come up against words or behavior that are unwanted, unproductive, and have no place in an effective and pleasant environment. "I" messages allow you to communicate about how something is affecting you (your emotions), while not blaming the other person and at the same time, encouraging them to take responsibility.

There are three elements to an "I" statement:

Behavior: Describe what is happening around you or what the other person is doing.

Feeling: How does the person's behavior make you feel?

Consequence: What happens as a result?

For example, you might say: "When x happens, I feel y, because..."

Such messages are designed to flag something that isn't working, without it sounding too confrontational. Simultaneously, it highlights the area that needs focus, attention, and care to rectify.

In the following examples, one set in the context of the workplace, the other between a parent and teenage child, notice that while we're reflecting back how we feel, we're still operating from the other person's perspective, as evidenced by the use of "When you..."

"*When you* keep dismissing my ideas in that way, *I feel* really frustrated *because* it seems like you don't value what I have to offer."

"*When you* were late coming home and didn't answer my calls, *I felt* worried and angry, *because I* thought something bad had happened to you."

By using "I" statements, it prevents you from stumbling into petty tit-for-tat arguments with the other person and keeps the conversation grounded and focused.

Effective pauses

By being quiet and allowing people to vent their anger and frustration, you can sidestep a potential argument or confrontation, as you cannot influence them when they are experiencing a period of such intense emotion.

This technique is simply refraining from saying anything after the other person appears to have finished talking. You'll know how long to hold this pause because if it begins to feel slightly uncomfortable, you need to hold on for a few seconds more. If in doubt, stay quiet. This will likely feel unnatural to begin with, as we often find ourselves rushing to fill any silence. Pausing is also helpful if you're communicating with someone who's a deep thinker and requires time to process their thoughts into coherent comments.

Pausing for a few extra seconds encourages the other person to keep on talking and provide additional information. I've seen this put to great effect when police officers interview suspects, witnesses, or victims who seem to feel obliged to fill the silence. Try it next time you find yourself in an argument.

Inexperienced communicators will often find themselves asking a question and, when no immediate response is received, will follow up with another question or prompt. We've all been there! To this day, I still keep a stress ball on my desk with the letters W. A. I. T. emblazoned on it as a reminder to ask myself: "Why am I (still) talking?" before I jump in.

Summarizing

Like paraphrasing, summarizing involves offering your understanding of what the other person has just said, ideally by using *their* wording, rather than your own, as you might do in paraphrasing. Doing this helps clarify the main issues or any information the other person has shared and helps build rapport.

This technique is best used in a conversation when a lot of information has been shared or one side has delivered a long, often rambling narrative about a perceived unfairness in the workplace, for example. By summarizing, it takes all of what they've just said and condenses it into a manageable chunk. For example, you might begin: "If I understand you correctly, what you're saying is . . . ? Have I got that right?"

This, in turn, provides clarity and focus to the real issues. It also allows you to keep track, remember what is being said, and buys you valuable thinking time to prepare what to say next. Don't get too caught up in remembering whether to paraphrase or summarize. All it boils down to is reflecting back to the other person the main points of what they have told you, which then allows them to correct you if needed, while also reminding both of you what the main points of the conversation have been. You could see summarizing as a combination of paraphrasing (what they said) and labeling (how they feel about it).

Remember, all of these active listening skills are not designed to be treated as a box-checking exercise or to be followed in a rigid format. Rather, they are tools that, with regular practice and flexibility in how they're applied, will enhance your ability to demonstrate level-five listening and communicate even more effectively, regardless of the circumstances.

What follows is an example of a workplace conversation between a boss and one of his team supervisors following recruitment challenges in the organization. It uses all of the above techniques:

The boss speaks first: "It sounds like doing a good job means a lot to you?" (*emotional label*)

The team supervisor replies: "Yeah."

"You seem reluctant to talk about it, though. Sounds like I may have misinterpreted an issue here?" (*label*)

"It's just frustrating to see people being hired without the right experience or knowledge, just to meet arbitrary targets."

"Without the right experience?" (*reflection/mirror, with upward inflection*)

"Yeah. They may have a degree, but most of them lack any common sense or real-world experience."

"How does this impact you directly?" (*open question*)

"It makes my job as their supervisor even harder than what it already is."

"Mmm..." (*minimal encourager followed by effective pause*)

"And it's the customer who ultimately suffers because they don't get the best service."

"What I'm hearing you say is, you feel that we're possibly not recruiting the right people and are allowing anyone in just to hit some random target. And this will have a negative impact on the job and create extra work for you?" (*paraphrase/summarize*)

(Continued)

> "Yeah, that's right. But what do you know about it? You haven't done the actual job yourself for years!"
>
> "Hang on. When you speak to me like that, I feel frustrated and angry, because I'm making efforts to try to understand what's going on so I can do something about it for you." ("*I*" *statement*)
>
> "I'm sorry. It's been a really difficult few weeks."
>
> "Sounds like it's been tough for you. Shall we work on a plan together to sort this out?" (*label*)
>
> "Thanks. That would be helpful."

Empathy and compassion

In chapter 1, we covered the concept of empathy and how important it is to effective negotiation. It's worth revisiting briefly here, as the ability to empathize with another human being is the cornerstone of active listening, not to mention a core competency of great leadership. Think of a recent conversation you had with someone in which you felt you weren't being listened to. This person's lack of empathy may have shown up as them blaming or shaming you, or refusing to listen to your point of view, holding a grudge, or even accusing you of being oversensitive.

People often use the terms "empathy" and "compassion" interchangeably. This is understandable, as there are many definitions of both, based on whichever school of thought the person favors. When it comes to communication, though, and more specifically negotiation, which one should you prioritize over the other? Well, the answer isn't as straightforward as you might think, because to become a world-class communicator you need both, depending on the context and circumstances you're facing.

If you are dealing with a suicide intervention and want someone to come down off a roof, you are not going to introduce yourself and then immediately suggest what route they should use to come down without first dealing with their emotions and maybe exploring some of their concerns.

For those who have to care for small children, watching them throw a tantrum on the supermarket floor, kicking and screaming because they couldn't have the candy or shiny thing they spotted on the shelf, will be familiar. At that moment when the child is in full flow, can you really problem-solve and get them to acknowledge that their behavior is inappropriate? No way. The child literally can't hear you, let alone accurately interpret the words you're saying, because they are too emotional.

When people are emotional, they're physically unable to listen and understand what you're saying. Plus, they don't want to listen, because they're not yet feeling seen, heard, and understood by you. You have to deal with these emotions before you can even begin to start problem-solving.

Their underlying emotions could be: "I am angry and frustrated about what happened." Or there may even be further subtle, latent, and hidden emotions. The more you can truly actively listen, the more you'll be able to uncover them.

As highlighted throughout this book, the golden rule of effective communication is *it's not about you*. Therefore, to gain another person's cooperation and maybe influence a change in their behavior, you must first connect with them and obtain an understanding of their world. In other words, you must demonstrate empathy, and the only way to do that is by physically doing it. In the MOREPIES section above, we covered some of the ways in which you can begin to do so.

There are lots of misconceptions about what empathy is and what it isn't. I imagine if you sat down a bunch of therapists, life coaches, negotiators, and the like, they'd all come up with their own definitions, spending hours debating the nuances, but in the end, they would look similar, yet still different.

In *Beyond Winning*, the director of the Harvard Negotiation Research Project Robert Mnookin and his coauthors neatly define empathy in the context of negotiation as "the process of demonstrating an accurate, nonjudgmental understanding of the other side's needs, interests, and perspectives." There's more, though. The most effective negotiators are able to strike the right balance between empathy, as just described, and assertion in their communications with others.

The difference between empathy and compassion

The concept and practical application of empathy and compassion are not new and have been with us for thousands of years. The evolutionary biologist Charles Darwin is well known for supposedly coming up with the term "survival of the fittest." In fact, it was Herbert Spencer, a scientific colleague of Darwin's, who was responsible for this idea, which credits competition for humankind's evolutionary success. Darwin, to the contrary, argued in his "sympathy hypothesis" that cooperation has played a bigger role in ensuring our success as a species. What Darwin called sympathy today would be termed empathy or compassion.

It's fair to say that both empathy and compassion are integral parts of the human condition, both of which enable us to thrive as a species. Both also allow us to connect with people by taking their perspectives into consideration, all while making better decisions that influence others. This is particularly important in times of crisis, conflict, or uncertainty.

Yet there is a difference between the two, and it's important to understand this, especially from a negotiation or leadership perspective. Being aware of this difference is what either creates that supportive, empowering workplace culture and closing meaningful deals with long-term clients, or failing to challenge poor performance and experiencing emotional burnout. Let's take a quick look at each one in turn.

Empathy helps you relate to others and build the relationships that lead to fulfilled lives. It is often described as being able to feel the emotions of another person; not just an awareness of them, but an understanding of what they may be experiencing. The reality is more nuanced, though. To take on the feelings of others can impact your own emotions in a negative way. Left unchecked, empathy can easily lead to you experiencing an "empathetic or emotional hijack," closely followed by feelings of being overwhelmed and burned out. This type of empathy is often referred to as "emotional empathy" and best describes what most people think of when they hear the term.

Another form of empathy is called "cognitive empathy." As a kidnap negotiator, I would regularly utilize "cognitive empathy" over its emotional cousin to enable me to understand the other person's perspective. Crucially, I could then reflect that understanding back to them, without the burden of feeling similar emotions to them. Cognitive empathy is closely related to emotional intelligence and is more of a skill you can learn, whereas the emotional variety is often instinctive and should be handled with care.

This doesn't mean I was devoid of any feelings, though. Far from it. I simply couldn't afford to take on any of the emotional burden and stress of others. I owed it to the families, the client, and, above all, the hostages to remain calm, focused, and engaged with the kidnappers.

If used correctly, empathy is a powerful communication tool. If you're not careful, though, it can also lead to cognitive biases. For example, you may find it easier to empathize with those who are more like you than with others who are not. This condition is evident in everyday politics and business, where we can feel extremely empathetic to the people on our own side, but less so to the opposition.

Empathy is often described as the precursor to compassion; you have to walk through empathy to get to compassion.

Compassion is best described as the ability to be mindful of the suffering of others, yet at the same time not becoming immersed in it. Doing so essentially provides you with an emotional firewall that allows you to take action.

Too much compassion, however, can lead to "compassion fatigue," which is frequently seen in professions like the emergency services and psychotherapy. People who struggle with this may also experience feelings of anxiety and an inability to focus.

Properly balanced, both emotions will make you a better communicator or negotiator. Empathy is a powerful part of being human, but left unchecked, it can get in the way. Compassion, on the other hand, will encourage you to take action to relieve the suffering you see. Be aware, however, that if you do too much, it's easy to forget to take care of yourself. Ultimately, the difference between the two is less important than your ability to develop and apply both skills when it counts.

Remember, empathy is *not* sympathy, which is when you're almost pitying or feeling sorry for the other person. It also doesn't necessarily mean agreement. Out of the many negotiations with kidnappers I've been involved in, it's fair to say that I didn't have much in common with them. I certainly didn't like them very much as people, especially when, as often happened, they put hostages on the telephone with their loved ones, forcing them to plead for their lives.

Yet it was crucial for me to be able to get inside their minds and understand how they saw and experienced *their* world. I didn't have to agree with them, I just had to try to understand that person, to not judge them or express subjective opinions or advice.

The other misconception about empathy is that it's all about being nice, gentle, and soft. It all depends on the context. There may be a time when that's appropriate—there are plenty of situations where I've had to display some deep empathy and rapport building, yet I was far from nice and cuddly. Empathy with people you don't like or have nothing in common with is not easy, but unless you spend sufficient time on this, you won't be able to move forward in your negotiation or build true rapport, which is the glue that binds it all together.

Rapport

In his book *Rapport*, forensic psychologist and University of Liverpool professor Laurence Alison argues that what is needed right now is a "rapport revolution . . . when we are able to extract someone's core beliefs and values, we often find that they are more similar to ours than we imagine. And when they are not, we don't have to agree but we should seek to understand."

He goes on to suggest that considering the following four questions in your interaction with others will establish a solid foundation for positive communication and human relationships:

1. Am I being *honest*, or am I trying to manipulate the other person?

2. Am I being *empathetic* and seeing things from their perspective, or just concentrating on my own point of view?

3. Am I respecting and reinforcing their *autonomy* and right to choose, or am I trying to force them to do what I want?

4. Am I listening carefully and *reflecting* to show a deeper understanding and build intimacy and connection?

Chapter Summary

Learn negotiation psychology and its practical tools and techniques to achieve success in all areas of your life.

CONTROL THE MESSAGE AND DELIVERY: While not every situation requires scripted conversations like those in a kidnap negotiation, it is important to give thought to what you want to achieve and convey a clear message for maximum impact and influence. By limiting communications to one voice, one method, and one consistent message, you ensure clarity and avoid conflicting information, resulting in a clear, impactful negotiation process.

OWN YOUR EMOTIONS: Emotions play a significant role in negotiations, and being able to regulate them is crucial. You are the architect of your emotions. They are not solely driven by a hardwired, fear-driven reptilian brain. They are shaped by your life experiences, bodily sensations, and interactions with others.

- Recognize that you have the power to choose your focus, interpret meaning, and determine your actions based on these emotions.

- Choose positive thoughts and emotions over negative ones and become skilled at recognizing and regulating both your own and others' emotions.

- Utilize BRAIN to discover and master the "four characters" of your brain and understand their dominance and the attention they require in your life.

EXERCISE PATIENCE: Patience is a superpower in negotiations. It allows you to slow down, think objectively, and make better decisions, especially in stressful situations. Developing patience helps you withstand uncertainty, be comfortable with discomfort, and avoid reactive patterns. Practice patience by taking a few seconds to gather your thoughts and consider your options before responding.

BALANCE YOUR NERVOUS SYSTEM: Managing stress and maintaining a balanced nervous system is essential for effective negotiation. To achieve this and avoid the "amygdala hijack," learn techniques to reduce stress responses and maintain optimal performance in real time, such as:

- Becoming aware of your bodily sensations

- Naming and acknowledging emotions

- Riding the wave of feelings without getting caught up in associated stories

- Breathing exercises like the physiological sigh and box breathing

- Exposure to cold therapy and prioritizing sleep

CREATE A GAP: When negative emotions, thoughts, and behavior impact on the quality of your communication, ask yourself the following three questions:

1. What am I focusing on right now? Is it the end of a relationship or a new beginning? Am I focusing on what's not going well or things that I can be grateful for?

2. What does this mean? You are a meaning-making machine, and the language you use to interpret and make sense of something will

determine the emotion or state you experience in that moment. Are you angry and frustrated, or concerned and understanding?

3. **What am I going to do?** Now that you've chosen your focus and given it its meaning, you'll then decide what to do, based on these two factors.

PRACTICE LEVEL-FIVE LISTENING: To influence and persuade others effectively, develop deep listening skills. Move beyond surface-level listening and strive for level-five listening, which requires focus and sensory acuity. Incorporate active listening techniques and MOREPIES (paraphrasing, "I" statements, emotional labeling, etc.) into your communications to enhance rapport and understanding.

Key Takeaways

1. Clarity is power. Be clear about what you want to say and achieve in your negotiations, and why doing so is important.

2. You are not a passive receiver of sensory input, but rather an active constructor of your emotions. We are feeling creatures who think, rather than thinking creatures who feel.

3. Balance your autonomic nervous system with simple yet powerful breathing techniques that will enable you to succeed in the most stressful of situations.

4. Five levels of listening are key to establishing deep rapport and trust-based influence.

When in doubt in any form of communication, always eat MOREPIES.

CHAPTER FOUR

Avoiding Common Negotiation Mistakes

I n this chapter, we will cover the importance of overcoming subconscious personal barriers and the (often deliberate) organizational blocks to communicating effectively that most of us experience at some point that obstruct true, empathetic listening. The topics we will cover are:

Technique 10: Personal barriers to effective communication

Technique 11: Deliberate blocks to effective communication

Technique 12: Embracing conflict: When resistance isn't always futile

We sometimes make these common mistakes during conversations, particularly when emotions are running high, such as problem-solving too early and failing to deal with emotions, both your own as well as the other person's.

Some of the reasons you might make these mistakes could be a lack of patience, a dislike of the person you are negotiating with, being tired, or dealing with your own emotions. You may be bored with what the other person is saying, or even worrying about the need for you to save face.

When people's lives are at stake, be it a kidnapping or some other crisis, effective communication with all parties involved is crucial. It's also a given that in the busy world we all live in, you won't always have the time, energy, or even the will to follow *all* the guidance contained in this book for *all* conversations. However, I would suggest that for those all-important conversations—such as with your loved ones, the workplace well-being conversation, the expensive purchase, or during conflict with a stranger— you try to follow as much of it as possible.

• • •

The following cyber-extortion case demonstrates how quickly things can escalate out of control, with potentially catastrophic consequences, if common communication mistakes aren't avoided.

Negotiation Case File #5: Asia-Pacific

The man was tired. Sitting at his desk in the open-plan, noisy office, he glanced at the time on his computer screen. Not long to go before the end of his fourteen-hour working day. The company paid him well, and his remit spanned most of the Asia-Pacific region, from India, China, and Hong Kong across to Indonesia, Malaysia, and Australia. But his stress was mounting.

He knew it wasn't worth speaking to his boss about the company's always-on performance culture, as nothing would change. He had accepted the fact that he needed to look for a new job. Working his way quickly through the last of that day's seemingly never-ending emails, the man prioritized anything that looked remotely interesting or important. He opened one marked "invoice—urgent," as it appeared to be a routine request for payment of outstanding fees, which he usually authorized. Clicking on the attached document, he thought the sender must've sent him the wrong one, as the invoice was for a company he didn't recognize. Thinking nothing of it and that it was a problem for tomorrow, he logged off his computer and braced himself for the long commute home.

Unbeknownst to him, by opening the attachment, he had enabled a hacker to remotely install a keystroke logging software program into the company's IT system. Over the next two weeks, the hacker would be able to roam freely and undetected through the system, accessing and stealing commercially sensitive information as well as the personal and financial data of thousands of employees.

Once the hacker had finished extracting the data, he launched a devastating ransomware attack, effectively encrypting close to four thousand computers and dozens of critical servers. Once they became aware of the problem, the IT team immediately shut down the network and attempted in vain to restore the system from the backup files, but to no avail. Twenty-four hours later, a ransom demand was received for $4 million in cryptocurrency in exchange for the decryption keys and the deletion of all the stolen data.

As this is happening, I'm on the other side of the world sitting at my own computer, reading the overnight updates on the other crisis response cases my fellow negotiators are deployed on. My phone vibrates, and I step into a spare conference room to take the call. I gaze out of the floor-to-ceiling glass window over the heart of the City of London with the distinctive Lloyd's Insurance building towering over it.

The stressed senior executive on the other end of the phone explains what has happened and wants urgent advice on what he should do next. The company can't access any client data and is losing vast sums of money each day they are locked out of their IT system. He drops into the conversation that they have seventy-two hours to pay the ransom, or it will double every twenty-four hours.

Using plenty of active listening skills and empathy, I reassure him that I understand the seriousness of the matter and that, however unlikely it looks right now, it is resolvable without making the multimillion-dollar payout. I then provide him with a list of options with pros and cons for each one, followed by a recommendation, and offer to speak with him the following day.

Two hours later, I'm in the back of a taxi on the way to the company's London office to meet with the chief information security officer (CISO), who happens to be in the country. He's not a happy man, and it's clear he's looking to avoid taking the blame for an incident that sits squarely within his remit. To make matters worse, the senior management team can't agree on a strategy, despite me offering up several tried and tested options. Specifically, they can't agree on whether they should begin negotiating with the extortionist, even if it's just to buy time to enable the technical guys to fix the problem. Not to mention gaining the time to make all the necessary mandatory notifications to relevant stakeholders, as well as gathering all the funds required to pay the ransom. All of which takes time. The very thing they didn't have.

Walking into the CISO's office, it's obvious from his tense body language that he's angry and looking for a fight, rather than finding a solution. I can sense it's likely driven by fear and a primal need for certainty and control, not to mention a desire to feel significant and save face. As the meeting progresses, I begin to form a picture of what it must be like to work not only for him but for the company as a whole.

What is evident is that the culture is based on fear, and failure of any sort isn't tolerated. This acts as an obstacle to employee creativity and discourages effective and bold decision-making. Unless an organization strives for constant improvement undertaken in an open, learning, and empowering way, then long-term business success is blocked and capable employees vote with their feet.

Eventually, wiser heads within the senior leadership team prevailed and it was decided that the disruption was costing the business too much; a swift resolution was required. This involved opening communications with the extortionist in order to buy time to enable a technical solution to be found.

Once we'd proven the extortionist's intent and capability, it was crucial for the negotiation to focus on building trust so that at the end of the negotiation, he'd feel adequately compensated for his enterprise and would not ask for more money (called "being doubled") or carry out the threat through spite or for revenge. This is achieved counterintuitively, by resisting, where necessary, the extortionist's demands and by reducing expectations early on. Only once this necessary confrontation has occurred is any meaningful progress likely.

However, two things distinguish the bargaining framework in a cyber-extortion case from a physical kidnap-for-ransom case and restrict our ability to negotiate as effectively, leaving us with little option but to pay a ransom amount. The extortionist has already got the data and has the power to publish it or refuse to provide decryption. They usually set a time limit as well. Furthermore, in any cyber-extortion, there are no guarantees that decryption will be provided, or any data obtained illegally will be destroyed or deleted once a payment has been made.

The negotiation strategy then becomes one of convincing the extortionist to settle the deal in a way that will be mutually advantageous. They could accept less than they are asking for and avoid any further action from law enforcement, hold out for more and possibly get caught, extend the deadline, or accept payment over a longer period.

However, in most cyber-extortion cases, and if the negotiation has been conducted diligently and with resolve, the chances of revenge or being doubled drop significantly once a payment has been made.

This case was eventually resolved by paying a tiny fraction of the initial ransom demand, yet it still took the company months to get back on track and cost it millions in lost revenue. If the company had established a more transparent organizational culture by identifying and then removing some of the communication blocks and barriers within the business, it might have avoided the whole situation in the first place.

● ● ●

Technique 10: Personal Barriers to Effective Communication

All of the following are examples of personal barriers to effective communication. Most of them aren't deliberate attempts to undermine what someone is saying; they are fired off subconsciously. This doesn't give us free rein to avoid responsibility, because through this book you now have greater awareness and can be more conscious of avoiding these stumbling blocks in the future.

Know-how: How good are you at handling a stressful conversation that involves conflict or emotion? Some people avoid dealing with people who are crying, because they feel like they never know what to say: "What if I say the wrong thing and make it worse?"

Effects of stress: There is a danger of cognitive ease when you are under stress, as you seek out what is familiar, easy, and validated by your preexisting beliefs. If you are angry or tired, you might be reluctant to listen effectively to another's viewpoint. For example, coming home after a long, stressful day at work, you are tired and hungry, but your partner wants to have a conversation about their landscaping ideas for the garden or their holiday plans.

Identifying/bragging: You refer everything the other person says to your own experience.

"I did that, but mine was much worse."

Advising: You are the great problem-solver, ready with help and suggestions.

"What you need to do is this and then that."

Experience: If you've had some experience of a particular type of situation, you may become overconfident in handling difficult conversations, plunge in too quickly, or shoot from the hip with your judgments. This barrier is about problem-solving too soon: "Let's get it over with. I am right, you are wrong." You think you understand the problem because you know the person, so therefore you presume to know what they are thinking and feeling: "Upset again, are you?" This can come across as passive-aggressive.

In kidnap or hostage negotiation, you may be the one highly experienced person on the ground dealing with the crisis, but you have a team supporting you. Make sure that your own emotions and mindset are where they need to be, by not becoming overconfident, yet at the same time avoid overthinking things.

Conversation or decision avoidance: Are you one of those people who never really has a meaningful conversation with anyone? Maybe you want to get everything exactly right and can spend too long gathering information. You might have a fear of what could happen. You might be distrusting of support, fear conflict, and expect others to help. For example, in the workplace, this could be a staff member whose performance needs addressing or, at home, your loved one has a personal habit that infuriates you, but you avoid having the conversation that you know, deep down, has to happen.

Analysis paralysis: You have too much information and detail, which in turn can cloud your thinking during the conversation. It's another form of avoidance too, always seeking more and more information to delay the inevitable.

Presentation: This barrier is well summarized in the saying "lies, damn lies, and statistics." Consider how the information is presented. People can easily put their own slant on information that influences how others think about it. This is known as the "framing effect," a form of cognitive bias in which the brain makes decisions about information depending on how it is presented.

For example, if a weather bulletin tells you there's a 40 percent chance of rain tomorrow or the teacher mentions that 40 percent of students fail the course you've just signed up for, most people will dwell on this aspect, rather than considering there's a 60 percent chance of it not raining or you passing the course.

Position in the relationship: Do you feel equal in the relationship? How do you deal with the behavior of demanding, judgmental, or powerful people? Do you feel superior, equal, or inferior? "Who am I to speak to this person?" Or it can manifest as, "I'm better than they are; therefore, I can speak to them in a different way."

This will have an impact on how you negotiate, as it brings with it subconscious beliefs about being "good enough" and your self-worth.

Quality of information: This entails going into a conversation with assumptions and opinions, but few facts, which can lead to misunderstandings, usually because of a lack of empathy or desire to discover the other person's "model of the world" as they see it.

Failing to learn: Not all conversations end well. It is important to reflect on your performance. This is why, in the negotiating world, you debrief after every incident. You look at what worked well and what didn't. You must seek constant improvement in the unrelenting pursuit of excellence. How many times do you do that in your day-to-day life, including in the workplace?

Other barriers to effective communication

Another barrier to effective communication is allowing our habitual, automatic language patterns, thought processes, and behaviors to rule the show. Because you are a leader, of yourself, if not others, you must go first by taking full responsibility for your thoughts, feelings, and behaviors, rather than blaming others for them.

Further barriers to effective communication can include thinking you're able to make people do something *you* want them to. If you have children, you will be given regular reminders of how futile this approach is when entering a negotiation with them. How often have you punished your kids for not doing what you wanted them to do? Did it result in long, emotional, drawn-out arguments, often followed by regret and remorse about some of the language used and words or actions that can't be undone or taken back? By being more conscious and aware of what you're feeling, saying, wanting, and what your triggers are, it will enable you to ensure your needs are being met while at the same time acknowledging and working toward helping the other person meet theirs.

It is easy to be triggered, particularly when communicating with others. In fact, all day long, you're likely to be subjected to constant trigger points if you don't stand guard at the door of your mind. Trigger points can include rolling news channels, scrolling social media posts, the pings of email and message notifications, a chronic urgency culture within the workplace, simmering disconnect with a significant other or colleagues. Unsurprisingly, unless you can handle such triggers in an appropriate way, they are likely to impede your ability to communicate or negotiate effectively.

Every time someone or something triggers you, causing an emotional reaction, pay close attention to where it is showing up in your body. Get curious and ask yourself better questions. Is it that you want to be seen as successful? Or is it more a case of losing face if you don't seal that business deal, thereby denting your ego and reputation?

Remember to step into the unpleasant emotion or thoughts. Feel the feeling and drop the story. And then thank the person or circumstance that brought it about (perhaps in your head rather than verbally), because it has shone a powerful light on the parts of your mindset and emotions that require attention. When we can drop any form of blame toward the other person for causing this, only then can we begin to communicate more authentically and empathetically. Anything else is just noise and clouds our ability to achieve connection and rapport with the person with whom we're negotiating. Only by really hearing their deeper needs and our own through this noise are we able to bring about trust-based influence and behavior change in another.

In particular, the way in which you might easily judge others is a surefire obstacle to a successful negotiation. How often have you found yourself labeling a colleague who appears more focused on the report's supporting data than you are as being "picky" or "pedantic"? Yet when you're more interested in such details than he is, you might label him as being "unfocused" or "sloppy"? When you can develop an awareness of such judgment and acknowledge that it is merely an expression of your own needs and values, your ability to communicate at a higher level is realized.

Have you ever been stuck in a conversation and felt bored, allowing your concentration to wane as your thoughts drift off to what you fancy for dinner or that email you must send before the end of the day? Chances are, though, what bores the listener also bores the speaker. If you're in the middle of a negotiation and you feel like it's just not going anywhere, remember the process of bringing it back on track.

One way of doing so is interrupting the speaker. Yes, you read that correctly. Sometimes we've just got to step right in there and halt the decline.

I do this with my coaching clients frequently (having got their permission up front to do so, of course!) if I sense that they're stuck in a disempowering language or thought pattern.

As long as I approach it with the right intention, this does not come across as rude or disrespectful; instead, I am doing it to empathize and understand their needs, feelings, and requests. Interrupting them also enables them to connect more fully to what they're saying and therefore develop clarity and focus, ultimately leading to a successful outcome.

One highly effective way of halting the decline is to ask them a question. Often, the more random or outrageous the question, comment, or action, the better. For example, if the other person is going round and round in their story, you could ask them:

"Do you like watermelon?"

They are likely to respond with something like, "Eh?"

"I said, 'Do you like watermelon?'"

"Um . . . yeah, I do."

Such a random question has interrupted their flow, which then gives both of you an opportunity to get the conversation back on track, but from a far more empowering place.

If we also interrupt with empathy and use an emotional label, it can have the same positive effect. For example, "It sounds like you're really frustrated with what happened in the meeting and that you felt like your opinion wasn't listened to or valued." This kind of interruption is likely to get the conversation back on track rather than drifting aimlessly, which is of no use to either of you.

Technique 11: Deliberate Blocks to Effective Communication

We've covered some personal barriers, which are largely subconscious, but there are also more deliberate blocks people use. These are often seen in the workplace, and, at times, we are all guilty of using them. Blocks are also sometimes organizational, usually in the guise of systems, processes, or a pervading culture. The extent to which any blocks are present will undoubtedly correlate with the example set by the managers and leaders within the organization. There is often an expectation that you negotiate as your manager or leader does.

There may also be an expectation for you to be like them, as people often employ others because they are like themselves. This is known as the "horns and halo effect," a cognitive bias that causes you to allow one trait, either good (halo) or bad (horns), to overshadow other traits, behaviors, actions, or beliefs. So you may feel pressured to negotiate in the same way as your boss, as it's the only way you can make them understand you.

Both personal barriers and deliberate blocks can obstruct effective communication and get in the way of developing rapport, achieving consistent high performance, or closing a deal. Consider the following questions to determine whether there are any blocks in your organization:

- What is the level of support offered to you when you have to have difficult conversations with your teams? Is appropriate training offered to fully prepare you? Do you have the right physical environment to have these conversations?

- How about the ethics, values, leadership styles, and culture? Do they enable or hinder effective communication? Is there a strong, pervasive sense of psychological safety?

- Do people shout at others across busy offices? Is there a "macho" or "toxic" win-at-all-costs culture?

- How do you hold meetings? All online and remote? Held in open-plan or small offices? How does this impact the quality of the communication?

- Is there a chronic urgency culture, underpinned by micromanagement and high workloads?

When you add these to the personal barriers we discussed above, you can see how much organizational culture can get in the way of effective communication. And, just when you might think these were enough, consider the negative impact if you also add the following into the mix.

Further blocks to effective communication

Dreaming: You half listen, and something the other person says triggers a chain of associations of your own. Too many minimal encouragers—"*and?,*" "*really?,*" "*uh-huh,*" "*hmmm . . .*"—can be evidence of this.

Derailing: You suddenly change the subject. You derail the train of conversation when bored or uncomfortable, or you joke it off.

Placating/Fake empathy: You want to be seen as nice, pleasant, and supportive. You want people to like you. You half listen, probably enough to get the drift, but you are not really listening to what is being said—"*Right, right . . . ,*" "*Absolutely . . . ,*" "*I know . . . ,*" "*Of course you are . . . ,*" "*Incredible!,*" "*Yes . . . ,*" "*Really?*"

Mind reading: You are trying to figure out what the other person is really thinking and feeling, rather than listening with an open awareness.

Rehearsing: Your attention is on the preparation and delivery of your next comment, which of course you believe is far more interesting than what you are currently listening to.

Filtering: You listen to some things and not to others, only the bits that interest you, or can link to your story.

Judging: You don't listen to what they say, as you've already judged them (they are boring, opinionated, etc.).

Obstacles to reaching a negotiated agreement may also include:

- Unsatisfied needs

- Fear of losing face

- Not vested in the solution

- Not ready for an agreement

- Inclination to resist perceived aggression

- Feeling aggrieved

- Sense of being misunderstood/mistreated

Here are some common mistakes:

- Problem-solving too soon (before empathy).

- Failing to *earn the right* to be critical or to advise. First, we need to convince the person that we *understand* their problem and *how they feel* about it.

- Failure to use active listening skills.

- Too much talking, interrupting, speculating on the other's experience based on your self-interests.

- Jumping to conclusions and displaying a judgmental attitude, which is a lack of empathy.

What can you do to prevent some of these things from happening?

The following Communication Sequence is the foundation of all hostage and crisis negotiations worldwide and is based on the negotiation stairway model designed by the former head of crisis negotiations at the FBI, Gary Noesner. Based on proven best practice established in the psychotherapy and counseling professions, it is designed to bring about meaningful cooperation and behavior change in another person. To achieve this, you must go through a specific sequence of steps in order, and you must spend sufficient time on each step before moving on.

As you can see in figure 4-1, the sequence starts with active listening. This could include identifying and labeling the other person's emotions, mirroring some of their language, asking open questions, listening with an empty mind rather than waiting for your turn to speak. Active listening is followed by demonstrating empathy—showing a willingness to understand other perspectives—then building rapport and establishing trust-based influence, which results in behavior change.

FIGURE 4-1
_____

Communication Sequence

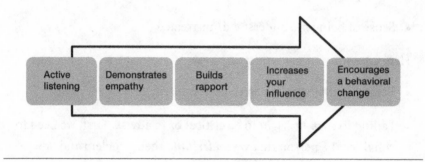

_____

By taking each step in turn, it allows us to break down any barriers to communication and ultimately bring about the change we want in the other person. In a kidnapping scenario, this is the release of the hostage for an appropriate amount of money, in the shortest possible time, while minimizing the chances of the victim being targeted again. In everyday situations, if you're looking for cooperation or agreement from another person, it's worth spending time going through each stage of the sequence in order, rather than attempting to jump straight into problem-solving.

Technique 12: Embracing Conflict: When Resistance Isn't Always Futile

Resistance isn't always futile

One aspect of kidnap negotiation that people sometimes struggle with is the concept of resistance, in the sense that we won't agree to the kidnappers' initially high demands and will often refuse to offer any more money until the kidnappers have reduced their price substantially. People often struggle to understand this, particularly considering how important rapport building and empathy is in all forms of communication. No one has said you're going to do anything different; you are still going to remain calm, collected, and professional at all times.

Yet these various resistance points serve a crucial purpose for specific psychological reasons, as well as some practical ones. It's not just a case of us simply playing hardball to stroke our egos. What they do is manage the other side's expectations and signpost to them where we want the negotiation to end up. This is about saying "no" to the kidnappers, without actually saying the word "no." Rapport can still be maintained during times of heated conflict. How can you apply this concept of resistance to your everyday life? It might involve establishing clearer boundaries within your personal and professional relationships. It is also important to continue this resistance until you reach a stage that is often referred to as "squeezing the orange." This is the moment when the kidnappers believe that they have got every last penny out of us and that there is no more available, even if the reality is different. There is usually a cost-benefit analysis to be made by the kidnappers, as they'll only release the hostages when the cost and effort of holding them exceeds the benefits of letting them go.

In a case where the demand was $100,000, I might make an initial offer of $15,000, so the kidnappers are under no illusion that after a hard-fought negotiation, they may end up with $40,000 or $50,000 between them. Yes, the bad guys need to cover their costs and pay their guys' wages, but we're not going to be their golden ticket to a life of luxury in the Caribbean.

How do we achieve this?

In one of the first meetings with the family or CMT, I will ask them how much they are willing and able to pay. I remind them that we're talking about getting real cash on the table, not some theoretical figure. And that's just the start. Once a ransom amount has been agreed with the kidnappers, we then have to place the cash in several bags, which will then have to be handed over to the kidnappers at an agreed rendezvous point, which could be on a boat out to sea, in a jungle clearing, or by the side of a deserted road.

Rarely is there a simultaneous exchange of cash for hostages at the drop-off point. Kidnappers are likely to be at their most suspicious and nervous of any ambush to arrest or kill them. Instead, the hostages are usually released a few hours or even days later.

Often, the challenge I face is convincing the family or CMT that even if they could access all the money demanded immediately, we still need negotiation discipline and the courage to not pay it straightaway. Why? For the simple reason that if we pay too much, too soon, the kidnappers will think, "That was easy" and then a number of scenarios are likely to play out:

1. They take the money, release the hostage, and then kidnap them again or take another family member or coworker the following week, as they now perceive you as being an easy cash cow.

2. They take the courier who is delivering the ransom money hostage, thereby enabling them to demand even more money (and giving you the additional dilemma of negotiating for an extra hostage).

3. They take the money and say, "Thank you for the down payment. Now we're ready to negotiate." At this point, you've lost all your money, put a huge target on your back for future kidnappings, and find yourself in an even worse position than you were when you started!

One of the best techniques to overcome these problems is to use a form of negotiation often referred to as "decreasing increases." For example, the initial demand is for $1 million, but the family or company are only willing and able to pay $100,000. This is called our target settlement figure (TSF), the final amount we want to close the negotiation at. So we might make an initial offer anywhere between 30 and 40 percent of the TSF. This is purely a guide and is by no means fixed in stone, as there are many variables that can impact this. Basically, we need to offer enough to keep the hostages alive, while at the same time signposting to the kidnappers where the negotiation is likely to end up.

Furthermore, increases often mirror the decreases offered in the kidnappers' demands. If they reduce the sum they are willing to accept by an unacceptably small amount, we always have the option to stick at our current offer. Or we may offer an unacceptably small increase to signpost to them, once more, that if they wish us to offer effective increases, they must also decrease appropriately.

Such "decreasing increases" are also ideally "ugly" numbers. For example, we will offer $27,473, rather than a nice round $30,000, as this is a more believable total amount of money held in a bank account. Our negotiation strategy usually focuses on creating a narrative of having to raise unpredictable amounts of money by selling equipment or from the goodwill donations made by family, friends, and the wider community.

Water off a duck's back

What is guaranteed is that the moment we put up any form of (necessary) resistance, we will experience some kind of threat in return from the kidnappers. This is usually in the form of a mock execution of the hostage or receiving verbal threats to harm the negotiator's family or even refusing to negotiate for weeks or months, with the silence and not-knowing often being the hardest element for the families to endure.

The kidnappers do this to test the family's or company's resolve and see whether they're telling the truth. It's easy to plead "We have no money" when everyone is being civil, but it's a different story when there is a credible threat of torture. Will the messaging remain the same or will the family panic? The communication must remain the same, otherwise it will likely extend the duration of the negotiation, which in turn only increases the risk to the hostages.

This is no different from any other area of your life. The moment you negotiate anything that might be remotely resisted by somebody, however good your intentions and no matter if it is the right thing to do, you're almost guaranteed to be on the receiving end of a "threat." This could take the form of an actual threat, a criticism, displeasure, blame, or being compared unfavorably to another. The secret is to not let it deter you from achieving your ultimate objective, whether that's freeing a hostage or standing up for something you feel passionate about, such as improving the performance of your team or department, moving on from a toxic group of people, or giving up your well-paid, yet unfulfilling job to follow your dreams.

What can help is having your own version of a properly considered and effective communications plan, which is fundamental to a successful resolution in any situation, particularly during a crisis. Crucially, this is different from the marketing or PR department quickly throwing together a press release. Having a plan in place enables you to withstand the inevitable threats and challenges that may come your way.

If you accept that such things are inevitable, you can plan and prepare for them, so when you do come under fire—and you will—you can respond appropriately and still retain that solid resilience to weather the storm. To do this as effectively as possible means you have to do more than just the "right thing." It's also about crafting the narrative that supports your actions, a positive narrative that is just as much about what you say to yourself as it is about what you say to others.

The communications plan might also include some talking points that we want to try to insert into the negotiations, reinforcing their importance in the minds of the kidnappers. We won't use a verbatim script, but it will be sufficiently detailed that the communicator can have some leeway in what they say, depending on whether the kidnappers are being cooperative or threatening.

Example of a kidnap negotiation narrative

- "This is a small, poor company. Trading conditions are very bad, and we have made a loss for the past two years. We don't have much money."

- "You are asking for an impossible amount of money. We cannot raise such a large amount."

This approach can also work in other forms of negotiation like dealing with your landlord, for example:

- "How can I pay the increase in rent you're asking for? I've been a good tenant for two years and I have a stable job, yet the rise in cost of living means I've got to count every penny."

Anticipated pressure points from the kidnappers

In response, we also want to consider the following points, similar to the Bunch of Fives we discussed earlier:

- Attempts to divide and rule by calling the families, friends, or colleagues of the hostage. We instruct them to ignore any such calls or direct the kidnappers to the dedicated number being used for the negotiation.

- Threats of harm to the hostages. Our response is always unequivocal; we will only pay if the hostages are well looked after.

- One of the most traumatic forms of pressure is when the kidnappers deliberately use silence, where they won't call. This is done to encourage the family or company to pay the ransom quickly when they do resume contact. One of the key roles of a negotiator is to reassure all parties that everything that can be done is being done. This is a particularly important thing to do with the families.

When we're attempting to get people to do what we want, in particular by punishing people for not doing something or for not keeping their side of the deal in a negotiation, we're ignoring the fact that true influence and behavior change is very much possible by taking a less confrontational approach. In his seminal book *Non-Violent Communication: A Language of Life*, Marshall B. Rosenberg describes how to do this by focusing on the following four areas of any communication:

1. Observations

2. Feelings

3. Needs

4. Requests

Let's apply his approach to an everyday negotiation you might find yourself in. For example, your teenage kids leave wet towels on the floor and your instinct is to shout, "How many times have I told you not to . . . ?"

According to Rosenberg, we must first *observe* what is happening in the situation. The secret here is to communicate this observation without any form of judgment or evaluation (implied or explicit). If you don't, you reduce the chances of them hearing your message, as they're likely to hear only criticism and offer only resistance.

Next, you might want to state how you *feel* when you observe this behavior. For example, "When I see your wet towel left on the bathroom floor, I feel frustrated and annoyed." We follow this by next articulating our *needs*, which are connected to the feelings. For example, "I need things to be left tidy in the bathroom, which all of us have to share."

Finally, the fourth aspect is to follow with a specific *request*, such as, "Would you be willing to place the towel on the rail or radiator once you've finished drying yourself?" Put it together and it will sound something like: "When I see your wet towel left on the bathroom floor, I feel frustrated and annoyed. I need things to be left tidy in the bathroom, which we all have to share. Would you be willing to place the towel on the rail or radiator once you've finished drying yourself?"

Can you see how much calmer and clearer this sounds than the usual ranting and raving that is so easy to fall into? The clearer you can be in all negotiations about what it is you want, the more likely it is you'll get it.

This also applies the other way too, when we're on the receiving end of another person's communication, particularly when we might already be categorizing them as "difficult." We can enhance our communication and connection by looking for the same four areas—what are they *observing*, *feeling*, *needing*—and then seek to understand what their real *request* is, which may be hidden behind some challenging emotions or behavior.

Requests versus demands

Is playing hardball a great strategy for negotiation? Not if you want to keep doing business with people, which after all is built on trust and honesty.

Relying on demands rather than requests rarely works, because negotiators are only human and often resort to the same tactic in response. This usually leads to a downward cycle of threats, demands, distrust, and even sabotaging the whole deal. When you receive a demand from someone, you've only got two choices: to agree or refuse, neither of which might be in your best interests. How do you overcome this?

Be mindful of whether your demands are being disguised as requests. One way this might happen is if the other side feels as if they would be punished or blamed if they didn't agree with it. To ensure your request doesn't become a demand by virtue of you blaming, shaming, or criticizing them for not agreeing, remember to demonstrate empathy toward their needs.

Drain the swamp of resistance

You're sitting in the conference room waiting for the presentation to begin or the boss to make an announcement, and you're not happy. You have a million and one other things to do that day and you'd rather be anywhere else. As they walk to the front of the room and begin to talk, you fold your arms subconsciously in an almost teenage demonstration of defiance.

"Thank you for being here. I know you're really busy and probably thinking, *I don't know how this is relevant to me or why I'm wasting my time here. She doesn't know the first thing about how to run this team.* You may also be thinking, *I wish she'd hurry up so I can get back to my desk.* It must be frustrating for you right now with all the challenges facing the business."

You unfold your arms and lean ever so slightly forward, thinking, *Okay, then. It sounds like she understands and gets it. Let's hear what else she has to say.* What has the boss done here? By identifying, communicating, and acknowledging these likely perceptions, she is pulling the plug on all the possible challenges or criticisms that might have existed. Essentially, she's draining the swamp of resistance. Because if she doesn't do this, it doesn't matter how articulate or beneficial the business plan, proposal, or contract may be; you won't be fully engaged or buy into the process. It will also linger like a bad smell in the background, threatening to rear its ugly head when negotiations get too tense.

Intellectual understanding can obstruct empathy

To empathize fully with another person is not easy to maintain. It requires a level of presence, which is not helped by our rapidly dwindling attention spans. To empathize at the level required to communicate and succeed in a negotiation requires an ability to listen to the space in between the words and even the silence. You'd be forgiven for questioning the point of doing so.

However, how often have you listened to somebody and felt a disconnection between the actual words they're saying and the emotions you sense in either them or yourself? In the workplace, you might be sitting with a colleague who is sharing with you some bad news they've just heard. As a decent human being, you naturally feel for them and their struggle. Yet rather than offer them empathy, you might find yourself offering advice or even reassurance even if your colleague hasn't asked for it. There is a very real danger that by applying such an intellectual understanding of the problem, it blocks the level of presence required to enable empathy.

Do not underestimate the power of listening consciously when engaged in any form of communication. You don't have to be a trained therapist or negotiator to do this. The only qualification required is to be truly present to what's really going on for both you and the other person in that moment.

The following summary includes other examples of things that can prevent us from being truly present and able to empathize in all forms of communication.

Chapter Summary

If you learn how to identify your personal barriers to effective communication, which often arise subconsciously, as well as those entrenched blocks that are often found in the systems, processes, and culture of an organization, you'll be able to embrace communication conflict in a healthy way that allows you to keep your cool and still achieve negotiation success.

To do this, consider the following:

SELF-AWARENESS: Recognize and overcome personal barriers that hinder effective communication, such as impatience, biases, fatigue, and emotional distractions. Awareness is the first step to overcoming these.

ORGANIZATIONAL AWARENESS: Identify and address entrenched organizational blocks that impede effective communication. Seek to influence necessary changes within systems, processes, or cultural norms to create an environment that is more conducive to communication.

CONSTRUCTIVE CONFLICT MANAGEMENT: Conflict can be a natural part of negotiation. Embrace it constructively as an opportunity for growth and resolution. Overcome negativity and challenges from others in a healthy way by staying focused and composed.

COMMUNICATION SEQUENCE: Follow each step in turn: active listening, empathy, rapport building, trust-based influence, and finally cooperation. Give sufficient time to each step to foster effective communication. Spend sufficient time at each one before proceeding. Remember, this is a guide to navigate the negotiation path, not a strict process to adhere to.

NONVIOLENT COMMUNICATION: The following approach promotes understanding and constructive dialogue, particularly during challenging or confrontational conversations.

- *Observe* the situation without judgment.

- Express your *feelings* related to the situation.

- *Articulate* your needs related to those feelings.

- Make specific *requests* for desired outcomes based on your needs.

ADDRESS PERCEPTIONS AND RESISTANCE: Acknowledge that others may have perceptions or reservations about you, your ideas, or your proposals. Proactively engage in open discussions to address negative thoughts or resistance. By addressing these issues early, you create an environment for more effective communication.

ESTABLISH HEALTHY BOUNDARIES: Recognize the importance of setting and maintaining healthy boundaries in both your personal and professional life. Learn to say "no" without using the word itself when necessary. Courageously using appropriate resistance helps manage expectations and guide negotiations toward favorable outcomes.

Key Takeaways

1. Identify the blocks and barriers that are getting in the way of your ability to communicate as effectively as possible.

2. Don't rush to problem-solve. Spend time moving along the Communication Sequence.

3. When engaged in challenging or confrontational communication, focus on using the four nonviolent conflict areas of *observe, feel, needs, requests.*

4. Know your boundaries and when to stand your ground and resist.

CHAPTER FIVE

Negotiating with Difficult People

P ay the money or they die." When you're on the end of a phone and someone says this to you, it tends to focus the mind a little on how you're going to negotiate with them. I think in anyone's definition, a person who makes such a threat could be deemed "difficult" or, as I like to refer to them, "worthy opponents." Remember, our choice of words and language dictates the meaning we give something and therefore impacts on the quality of our emotions.

While it is unlikely you'll ever face somebody making these sorts of threats to you, not all conversations are easy, and the same principles apply to many situations. They are particularly relevant when you're going into a negotiation to face a person you've deemed to be a worthy opponent. In this section, I will show you how to deal effectively with highly emotional and stressful conversations, including learning the following techniques:

Technique 13: First, seek to understand. What is their model of the world?

Technique 14: Create a plan, then work the plan. "Risk" is not a dirty word.

Technique 15: Succeed in stressful, emotional, or sensitive negotiations.

This section also contains some useful techniques to deal with people who may demonstrate a lack of empathy or respect toward you, perhaps by dismissing any guidance or support you may be offering. It also covers ways to identify how the person you're communicating with views themselves in your relationship. Understanding this will enable you to alter your communication style to assist in rapport building and influencing.

When you're negotiating with "worthy opponents," unless you follow some basic guidelines, you can easily find yourself in a battle of egos. Therefore, your approach has to begin by stepping beyond an "us versus them" way of thinking and communicating. There's no place for an "I'm right and you're wrong" approach if you want to communicate consistently at the highest level.

Think about the last time you struggled to achieve the outcome you were seeking or didn't feel listened to. Chances are it was because one or both of you had this mindset. You might also have employed your old patterns of defending, withdrawing, comparing, or attacking if you felt judged or criticized in any way, however slight.

Feeding the ego

This is about communicating with another person who is allowing their subconscious operating system to run the show, while making sure you don't come off worse as a result. Feeding their ego is therefore a viable option. It's what they need, after all.

You must also be mindful to allow them to save face when this is necessary. People often don't mean to get themselves into situations or worked up and angry. One of the things that often prolongs the time criminals hold hostages inside a bank or keeps a person standing on a rooftop threatening to jump off is that they can't face coming down in the presence of their family or friends. They worry this will be seen as a weakness.

Imagine yourself in an argument when you are out with your friends or you're in a dispute with someone over returning a product to a shop. Your partner is with you, and they clearly want you to "win" the argument, making it hard for you to back down. That's when saving face can help, and removing the audience is one way of doing so. It's one of the reasons the police ensure the public are not near the scene when a negotiation with a person in crisis is taking place.

If you are to have a conversation where saving face might be an issue, consider removing the audience and maybe altering the immediate surroundings so the person you are talking to feels safer and more able to change their mind or acknowledge their emotions. As we've already highlighted, until a person feels safe in this way, they won't be able to regulate their emotions sufficiently to consider rational, objective thinking.

Technique 13: First, Seek to Understand. What Is Their Model of the World?

What and who do we mean by "difficult" people? I think you have some ideas about who you might class in this category. It usually means someone who is perhaps overly demanding or who projects a lot of ego. These people love to be in control and don't always sincerely value you or your contribution that much, treating you with little respect. You might find it difficult to be genuinely warm to them, as they may give you the impression that they think they are better than you.

However, you can't influence and persuade somebody—which, after all, is the desired outcome of all negotiations—if you're judging them. The old adage still rings true: first seek to understand where the other person is coming from, and why, before we even begin to think about getting them to understand our position.

Dealing with difficult people

Negotiating with difficult people can often include those people whose views, motives, and behavior you dislike or believe are completely "wrong." You may even distrust them. As we've covered elsewhere in this book, you must avoid letting your ego get in the way here and find the opportunities wherever possible to create value and progress in the negotiation that you find yourself in.

While there are well-known strategies out there that might help you achieve your negotiation goals, such as BATNA (best alternative to a negotiated agreement—what's your alternative endpoint if negotiations fail?) or ZOPA (zone of possible agreement—common ground all parties can agree on), most of these strategies ignore the fact that human beings don't negotiate or make decisions rationally and objectively, despite us thinking that we do.

In a kidnapping case, for example, rarely, if ever, will you be negotiating with a rational, open-minded, objective individual. Nor will the people on your side of the table be like this. When the stakes are high, emotions drive everything. Which is why mastering the art of emotional intelligence is so important in succeeding at negotiation. If you can't identify and manage both your own and the other person's emotions, it won't be a pleasant experience for anyone involved.

In his book *Thinking, Fast and Slow*, the Nobel Prize–winning economist and psychologist Daniel Kahneman explains how humans are not always in conscious control of their thoughts and actions and are therefore open to being influenced and persuaded. He further explains that we have two systems of thought:

> *System One* is impulsive, intuitive, and emotional.

> *System Two* is slow, deliberate, and logical.

He says that System One directly impacts what happens in System Two, which ultimately determines how we think, feel, and act. Therefore, if through our empathy and language we can affect the other person's System One, we can predict their System Two responses (i.e., their thoughts, feelings, and behavior).

It's worth reminding ourselves at this point that Kahneman's two systems are simply metaphors about how the mind works—in the same way as we think of our left brain as logical and right side as creative—rather than structures of the brain itself.

This point is highlighted by one of the world's leading neuroscientists, Dr. Lisa Feldman Barrett, who writes in *Seven and a Half Lessons About the Brain*: "Your brain does not 'light up' with activity, as if some parts are on and others off. It does not 'store' memories like computer files to be retrieved and opened later. These ideas are metaphors that emerged from beliefs about the brain that are now outdated . . . rather your brain is a network—a collection of parts that are connected to function as a single unit."

Sometimes succeeding with difficult people simply boils down to helping them save face. I've experienced this countless times in kidnap negotiations where if I try to humiliate or dismiss them, it's not going to end well for the hostages. I might not be offering any more money or concessions, but if I can park *my* ego, take a moment to gather myself and regulate my emotions, I can then help them save face and somehow make them feel they are getting their way. By doing so, I eventually achieve my ultimate goal, which is always the safe and timely release of the hostages.

As you know from the earlier section in this book on personal barriers, "conversation avoidance" and "know-how" are some of the things that get in the way of us having honest, empathetic, and effective communication. You tend to avoid these difficult conversations or you are not that good at them due to lack of practice. Either way, you usually come away from them feeling less than good about either yourself or the other person.

Ask yourself the question: How long can you shout at someone? One minute? If there is no reaction to the shouting, what happens? It can become about saving face, particularly if others are watching. Just remaining silent and allowing the person to vent can be enough. This technique can be highly effective on the telephone. What often happens if you remain quiet is the person will stop shouting and, if you remain quiet for a little longer, they will come back in and ask if you are still there. Quietly confirm you are listening. They may start up again, but this time it will be shorter.

Repeat this until their emotions are spent and you can begin the conversation, because calm, rational, objective thought (System Two) is now in the driver's seat. Remember, people can't truly listen when they are in a high emotional state (System One).

By way of refresher, one way of bringing more System Two into play is to label the strong emotions being lobbed at us, such as anger or frustration. Doing so allows us to level out the emotional balance referred to earlier. You can label it by saying things like, *"It sounds/looks/seems like [insert emotion here]."* Then stay quiet, rather than filling the silence with a "but" or "because."

This provides the other person with space to take in what you said as well as allowing them to clarify and verify their emotion. Even if you incorrectly label it initially, that's okay. Subconsciously, they will hear that you are attempting to see and understand things from their perspective.

You still have to show the other person empathy, even though you might not agree with the way they're speaking or even the content of their argument. While it is hard to show people empathy when you don't agree with their values, or when you're being shouted at, it's necessary to do so to build rapport. It's not always about being "nice."

A Quick Refresher on Cognitive Empathy

1. Empathy is not sympathy, nor is it necessarily agreeing with the other person or feeling what they're experiencing.

2. Empathy is identification of another's situation, motive, and emotion and communicating that back to them so they feel seen, heard, and understood.

3. Making the attempt to get it right is what is important.

4. Empathy creates a positive atmosphere for problem-solving.

5. It must contain no judgment and should acknowledge the other person's point of view.

Further considerations

Expect to receive demands

In difficult negotiations or conversations, you should expect to receive demands from the other person. Demands come in all shapes and sizes. They can be a kidnapper or hostage-taker who doesn't want to be arrested. Or, it might be someone in the workplace wanting to change shift patterns, move teams, or who is asking you to discipline someone they feel hasn't been performing as well as they should.

Position in relationship

There are ways you can establish what sort of person you are dealing with and how they see themselves in their relationship with you by the words they use. Specifically, do they see themselves as inferior, superior, or equal?

If someone says, "Look, you can't help me. I am at a loss. Whatever you say won't help. I wish I had your opportunities," it's likely that this person has low self-esteem and therefore probably sees themselves as inferior to you.

If someone says, "Listen, I know me. You don't know much about this at all. I know what to do. I don't need any of your advice," it's likely this person believes they are somehow better than you and are displaying signs of being governed by an unhealthy ego. They are likely to see themselves as superior to you.

Now, imagine yourself with a friend or colleague. You are genuinely praising one another for recent achievements or giving and accepting critical feedback. You are both open and in tune with what is going on for the other person. This equal position is where you should aim to be in all of your negotiations, a place of a mutual respect where you both feel as though your needs and outcomes are being met in the situation.

You can also identify this as the point where you are both actively listening, demonstrating empathy, and feeling good about yourselves. This is a flow state, requiring minimal effort. Ultimately, you want to leave people thinking they would like to continue doing business with you.

Convince them that any advice you do offer is to their advantage

Managers and team leaders sometimes have conversations with staff who may be considered "difficult" to deal with. These people are "worthy opponents," because they encourage us to step up and really tune in to their model of the world. For example, someone at work may not be performing as well as they should be, and when they sit down with you to talk about it, they may be reluctant to disclose the actual issue that's causing them to underperform. They may also dismiss your offer of support to take time out or reduce their workload, claiming they can deal with the problem themselves and are just notifying you out of respect in case you notice a change in behavior.

Other people may refuse to take your advice, full stop. In fact, they dismiss it completely, seeing it as a weakness to ask for emotional support. To get through to them, they must be convinced that your advice or proposal is to their advantage. One way of doing this might be to say:

> "By talking about your concerns, we can offer you assistance. It sometimes helps to share a problem, and we can refer you to more support."

Remember to praise their ability to make tough and realistic decisions. This might sound like:

> "It takes courage to talk about these matters."

> "It's brave of you to discuss your emotions and how you feel."

> "It takes strength to admit you have these dark thoughts."

> "It's your decision as to what assistance you require and take up."

You can feed the ego again at this point and allow them to keep feeling in charge, by saying:

> "You have the right to decline the support."

> "You decide what you want to discuss and what's important to you right now."

"You can stop the discussion at any time. Everything is confidential, and no one needs to be aware unless you wish to share."

If they are worried about others finding out about the issue, you might want to help them save face, as mentioned:

"Should you wish to change your mind or decline support, that's okay; no one will think less of you."

"You can tell the rest of the team other reasons for you changing shifts/taking leave at short notice."

During the Covid-19 pandemic, parents of teenagers often faced the difficult situation of their children wanting to break the rules to meet up with their friends. Parents then had the opportunity to use some of these techniques to great effect to help them cope with restrictions.

1. Raising their children's self-esteem by reminding them, "You have coped with lockdown so well up to now. You have kept your distance from your friends, which took great effort. Not everyone has managed to be so patient."

2. Convincing them your advice is to their advantage by saying to them, "By staying in and away from your friends just a little longer, you'll help keep your grandparents safe and save the lives of other vulnerable people. We, as your parents, will make sure you receive more of x or are allowed to y, if you do so."

3. Praising their ability to make tough decisions. "You have been prevented from enjoying your hobbies but managed to begin new ones. This shows great spirit and resilience."

4. Helping them save face with their friends who were out breaking the rules by saying, "It's okay to tell your friends that it was your parents who prevented you meeting up. You can tell them about the extra benefits or gains we have given you for not meeting up."

It's important to stress that the above examples are only a very small part of the negotiator's toolkit and you have to demonstrate a lot of active listening, as well as other techniques such as open questioning, deliberate pauses, and emotional labeling, for these strategies to be as effective as possible.

Technique 14: Create a Plan, Then Work the Plan. "Risk" Is Not a Dirty Word

Planning and risks

While most of you will plan for many things in your daily lives, such as holidays and business trips, few will actually take the time to plan a conversation, even when you know it is likely to be difficult. However, planning for difficult conversations will enable you to assess the risks more accurately and then take action to mitigate them.

Risk assessments are not an exact science. The future is uncertain and largely unpredictable, as are people. This is why many conversations involve risk. As a hostage negotiator, the risk may be a physical one, but in a private or work-based conversation, it can often be about a relationship or a reputation.

Imagine your friend has started a relationship with someone you believe to be totally inappropriate for him. You know that he is in love with her, but you also know that if you raise it as an issue, your friend might feel like he has to choose sides. It is the same when your kids start dating and you disapprove of their choice of partner. To avoid that possibility, you decide not to have the conversation at all, as you believe the risk is too great.

While this might be an option in your personal life, it's a luxury we don't have in a kidnap negotiation. It is therefore worth empowering yourself by conducting your own risk assessment before making a decision.

As a manager or leader in the workplace, it is highly likely you would have had to speak to a team member about poor performance. I remember, as a young police sergeant, I had to do just this on numerous occasions. In one instance, an individual's performance and behavior, while not exactly desirable, wasn't at a level to require discipline. He came across as arrogant and refused to take advice or accept that his performance needed improving in any way. Overall, though, he was an experienced and well-liked individual among his peers, yet still a classic "difficult" person to manage.

As I knew it was going to be a difficult conversation, I needed to plan beforehand. My ultimate outcome was for him to be a strong contributor and add value to the team. I needed to feed his ego just enough to convince him that any suggestions made were to his advantage, as well as praise his ability to make difficult decisions in fast-paced, critical incidents (which he was genuinely good at).

As part of the planning process, and being mindful of how easily personal blocks and organizational barriers can obstruct effective communication, these were some of my considerations I wanted to establish before I had the discussion:

- The purpose of the conversation.

- Likely content and talking points of the conversation.

- Previous conversations about the issue (establishing who was involved, when they took place, and what was said or requested).

- Previous relevant information or advice that has been given to the staff member that could have a bearing on the matter at hand (from their union, HR, medical, etc.).

- Do I need to gather further information before having the conversation?

- What information is already in the public domain?

- Who else knows about this meeting? Is there likely to be a need for this person to "save face" if it's widely known this meeting is taking place?

I also knew it was important to manage expectations and set an agenda beforehand with clear parameters. This also addresses the human need for control and certainty.

Remember to assess the risks. Consider whether they are too great to have the conversation right now, or, if you do intend to go ahead with the conversation, how can you mitigate the risks? Make a note of how you are going to convince them it's to their advantage, feed their ego, and praise their ability to make hard decisions. Ensure your own emotions are in check. Are you in the right mood? Label the emotions you see and any shifts. Consider everyone's basic needs. And try some effective silence. You may initially feel uncomfortable doing so, but when you take turns in a conversation, if it's their turn to speak, they will feel more pressure than you to fill the gap and keep talking.

Conversation planning

Before you even sit down to negotiate with your "worthy opponent," you might want to consider some of the following simple, yet effective questions to help in your planning process, based on those posed by Robert Mnookin in another of his books, this one called *Bargaining with the Devil*.

- **Interests.** What are my interests? What are their interests? Also consider these questions in the bigger scheme of things, such as, "What's important to me?"

- **Alternatives.** What are my alternatives to negotiation (or my desired main outcome for this conversation)? What are the other person's alternatives to the same?

- **Potential negotiated outcomes.** Is there a potential deal or outcome that could satisfy both parties' interests better than our alternatives to negotiation?

- **Costs.** What will it cost me (not just financially) to negotiate or to have this conversation? What are the long-term impacts of that?

- **Implementation.** If we do reach a deal, is there a reasonable prospect that it will be carried out or followed through?

Further considerations include:

- Who is best able to speak with the member of staff in a crisis?

- Have they experienced recent stresses or trauma?

- What is their availability and current workload?

- What is the frequency of contact required?

- Do they have previous experience of dealing with such conversations?

- Have you had any previous contact with the staff member or any relationship with them?

- What are the needs of the person?

- Consider gender or cultural issues.

Assessing and mitigating risk

Once you've identified the risks as part of your planning process, you'll need to know how to deal with them appropriately for the circumstances and context. For example, do you ignore the risk and carry on as intended or perhaps postpone the conversation indefinitely until you're satisfied that the risk no longer poses a threat?

Here are just a few ways to consider doing so:

1. **Tolerate the risk:** Carry on with the conversation without any mitigation, regardless of the risks to health, relationships.

2. **Treat the risk:** Set out boundaries; manage expectations and expected outcomes; agree on the criteria, content, timings, and locations.

3. **Terminate the risk:** Decline the conversation, walk away, or close it down with an explanation.

4. **Transfer the risk:** Obtain support from another, allow a colleague to take up the conversation. This person could be someone who has

perhaps demonstrated more influence with this person in the past or is currently in a calmer mood, has more time to spare, has more knowledge of the person or the current issue.

As you're going through this process and you realize there is a level of risk, consider whether the following behaviors are evident in yourself or the other person. If so, professional assistance *may* be required:

- Reliving traumatic events over and over. Flashbacks.

- Evident weight loss or gain. Digestive difficulties. Overuse of alcohol, etc.

- Depressed mood for a week or longer; nothing seems to help.

- Feeling on "red alert" constantly. Disproportionate anger.

- Limiting activities to avoid reminders of what happened.

- Anxiety that becomes hard to bear. Poor sense of humor.

- Guilt. Blaming others extensively. Difficulty connecting with family and friends.

- Sleep difficulties. Nightmares.

Technique 15: Succeed in Stressful, Emotional, or Sensitive Negotiations

This section introduces you to techniques to use during sensitive and delicate conversations. But what do we mean by stressful, emotional, or sensitive conversations? These conversations are the ones people often avoid because they're uncomfortable, even though they are necessary. Consider those times when you may have had to speak with someone despite feeling awkward about it because you weren't quite sure how to prepare or what to say. Or possibly when someone shared something that made you feel uncomfortable. Or those times where someone showed vulnerability, perhaps by disclosing something personal and private, such as a traumatic experience. It could also be a well-being discussion in the workplace.

This section includes a structure for you to follow when communicating with people where such situations are likely. You will discover:

- How to define basic human needs.

- How to satisfy the basic human needs in another.

- What causes stress before, during, and after such conversations.

- Words to use that can reduce stress.

- The importance of identifying and dealing with emotions.

- The importance of identifying your own emotions and needs prior to, during, and after such conversations.

When an individual's basic needs such as safety, self-esteem, and belonging are affected, a person will feel stressed and their emotions will be heightened. This prevents the building of rapport and, subsequently, any form of meaningful and respectful dialogue. Stress can also result in reckless actions that can affect the safety or success of others. This is why it's important to identify which of the other person's basic human needs are not being met in a conversation and how to address them.

In this section, you will also learn how to control the pace of the communication, prevent misunderstandings, and ensure accuracy. This is particularly important when communicating with people who may be classed as vulnerable through a disability or learning need, for example. It also avoids their answers being tainted by inappropriate, leading, or suggestive questioning.

• • •

Negotiation Case File #6: United Kingdom

A young man is sitting in a parked car in north London. He's holding his eight-month-old baby tightly to his chest, as if he doesn't want to let her go. The truth is he doesn't. No one doubts his love for his daughter, but despite her piercing cry, there's no way he's handing her back to her mother after a weekend of custody.

Hearing the baby cry in distress for such a long period naturally causes stress among the negotiators and other police officers present, who are using all the skills you've learned so far in this book to persuade him to unlock the car door and hand over his child. Everyone's stress levels are raised. The man is overwhelmed by his emotions, and he is angry and at the end of his tether. This frustration is directed toward the police and his ex-wife. The police are concerned that he might harm himself or the baby.

When people are stressed, it's often because their basic needs and wants are not being met. You may already be familiar with this idea from concepts such as Maslow's hierarchy of needs or Tony Robbins's six human needs. Essentially, what these concepts point to is that every human being on the planet, regardless of geography, culture, or language, is motivated by and striving for certain basic needs to be met. These include:

1. Safety, certainty, and control

2. A sense of belonging, love, connection, and achievement

3. Self-esteem, fulfillment, and self-actualization

It's vital to understand the difference between *needs* versus *wants*. Our need as negotiators is to get the man and his baby out of the car safely. We're not going anywhere until that outcome occurs.

This negotiation will not succeed, though, until we can uncover what *his* needs are. His wants are another issue altogether. He may *want* the police to just go away and leave him alone, but that's never going to happen. In reality, behind all the bravado and shouting, his primary human *needs* are simply to feel safe, secure, and in control. And, we have to meet those needs while balancing the risk to everyone else present.

In most negotiations, people don't express their needs outright. They might hint at them, but they'll rarely come out and say them directly. How do we uncover them? By moving slowly through the Communication Sequence, as covered above, with a healthy dose of MOREPIES thrown in, such as emotional labeling, mirroring, effective pauses, and paraphrasing.

Our man in the car is stressed because he has no idea how things are going to end in this scenario, so he has no certainty. He is also probably wondering whether the police are going to smash the window and drag him out, or is he going to get arrested and go to jail? He also has no control over events, as he is being prevented from driving away by the police. He may even think he will be injured if he resists police action, so his safety need is threatened. His baby being taken from him will also affect his sense of belonging, not to mention his sense of love and connection. When these needs are taken from us or are lacking, we feel stressed.

This not only influences your physical actions; it also impacts how you communicate. For example, you may know people who fly off the handle or say the wrong things, as difficult conversations become all about winning for them.

The man locked in his car holding his baby hostage is ticking all the boxes here: his basic human needs are not being met. He is stressed and he can't take flight, because he is trapped in a car. He is in fight mode, displaying his anger verbally, followed by freeze mode, which displays itself in the form of long periods of silence.

Our objectives here are twofold:

1. Address his needs to reduce the stress and defuse the fight.

2. Identify and label his emotions so we can deal with them.

A careful selection of words can remind the person how an alternative action might better satisfy their missing needs, while reminding them that these needs may already have been met, in fact. We must do all this with the understanding that the other person's reality may differ completely from our own.

By telling the man in the car that no one will harm him, that no one will force entry into his car, and that he will be looked after when *he* decides to come out, his physical needs for certainty and safety are satisfied.

Another golden rule in all kidnap or crisis negotiations is that we never tell a lie. Because to do so erodes all trust and makes it difficult to progress with the negotiation. We need to be honest about what is going to happen.

In this case, for example, we must be honest and say that under no circum-stances will the man be allowed to leave the scene with the baby. He knows he will eventually have to get out of the car and the police are not going to leave him alone until he does.

Yet despite all of this, we can still allow him to feel a sense of control. He is the one who makes the decision about when to unlock the car and get out. He decides on the timing and ultimately the health and welfare of the baby. While he does have control, he might have to be reminded of it, which in turn will raise his self-esteem.

His self-esteem and fulfillment needs can be met by encouraging him to think about the future and how good decisions taken right now can help him. This might include talking through other ways in which he can get to see his child. The more we address these needs or remind him of them, the more it is likely to reduce his stress levels.

He is, therefore, now more likely to take the time to think and listen and is less likely to commit any further reckless acts.

So, these are *his* needs. But before I think about them, I need to be acutely aware of how my *own* basic needs are affected. It's just like put-ting on your own oxygen mask on a plane before you help anyone else to do the same.

When someone shouts at you or appears threatening, you're confronted by a tirade of abuse and anger. What can happen then is you freeze and become immobile, unable to speak coherently, as you are shocked and over-whelmed. Your pulse rate and blood pressure increases, your pupils dilate, you shout back.

At this point, it's hard for anyone to converse at all, let alone use mean-ingful dialogue. You fear for your safety because you don't know how people are going to react to your behavior, creating a lack of certainty. Anger is an interesting emotion because it impacts both the giver and the receiver.

As a negotiator, there is always stress, but we work to reduce it. We do this first by addressing our needs to ensure we are safe; for example, by cre-ating physical distance between us and the kidnappers or hostage-takers. We also give ourselves an element of control by taking breaks when we need to. We have a great team around us that gives us a sense of belonging, and our belief in our training gives us self-esteem. Although we can't be certain how the negotiation will go, I know through experience that things usually turn out okay in the end so we get that element of certainty.

* * *

> TAKE TIME NOW TO THINK OF A SITUATION
> IN YOUR OWN LIFE WHERE YOUR
> NEEDS WERE EITHER MET OR NOT.

As negotiators, sometimes we get a chance to briefly speak to the hostages while they're still held captive. This is usually a great morale boost for them and their families, who get to know that they're alive and well, notwithstanding their circumstances. We always assume the kidnappers are listening in to the conversation, and we usually only have seconds—a minute at best—before the kidnappers cut the call. So, what do we say to them?

We can simply remind them of the importance of eating, drinking water, and exercising, if they get the chance. These activities will give them a sense of *certainty* and *control*. We tell them that their families and colleagues are doing everything to get them home as quickly as possible—thereby creating a sense of *belonging*. We praise them for how well they're doing, in order to build their *self-esteem*. Ultimately, it's about encouraging them to seize every opportunity to meet their own basic needs despite being in probably the most challenging situation they have ever faced in their lives.

Let's move this to a work environment. Think about a team member who didn't get that internal role they applied for and who now feels rejected; or the colleague who failed to get their bonus, and who doesn't have the best relationship with their boss and is now worried about getting sacked. How could you help them meet their basic needs?

How to Navigate Sensitive Conversations

Planning and environment

In sensitive conversations, you can expect emotions such as anger, frustration, sadness, regret, and many more to be present in both you and the other person. There are also likely to be some risks that might impact the success of the conversation. Additional time is likely to be required for you to practice sensitive active listening and questioning. Time spent at the planning stage will not go to waste and will likely enhance your ability to listen and understand.

It will also encourage the other person to be as consistent and complete in what they are able to recall and tell you about what happened or what they wanted to happen. This, in turn, will help you support them and meet their needs as effectively as possible. For example, you could signpost for them the most appropriate service for their needs, such as counseling or bereavement support if a close colleague has just died. Or they may have been overlooked for promotion and feel the process wasn't fair, and they simply want to vent their frustration to you and be heard.

Some further considerations:

- Who else knows about the situation or incident to be discussed in the conversation?

- Your current emotional state and that of the person you will be in conversation with. Do you have the energy and focus to give that person your full attention, knowing it is likely to be a challenging conversation?

- Any previous incidents that are relevant.

- Knowledge of the person you are talking to. You might not know them that well, particularly in a workplace setting.

- Knowledge of the incident that is to be discussed.

You've done the planning, now you have to think about controlling the pace.

Slowing the pace

When you're communicating with sensitive or vulnerable people, you need to remove the pressure on them as much as you can. One way of doing this is to slow the conversation right down, thereby giving them space to think and feel, without any pressure. By building in effective pauses—letting silence do the work—it can help control the pace of the conversation.

Here are some top tips to help you manage the pace:

- Slow down your speech rate.

- Allow extra time for the person to take in what has just been said or asked by you and provide time for the person to prepare their responses to your questions.

- Be patient if the person replies slowly or appears to be "rambling."

- Avoid immediately posing your next question.

- Avoid filling in the answers to questions for the person.

- Avoid interrupting.

In a kidnap or crisis negotiation, one of the main objectives, once the CMT has been established and everyone is ready, is to slow everything down, even for a short time, as this allows any anxiety, nerves, or stress to reduce while increasing the opportunity for objective, calm, rational thought. This applies as much to the kidnappers as it does to us. Now, this might seem counterintuitive. Surely you want to resolve the negotiation as quickly as possible? Yes, you do, but you want to do so in a calm, controlled manner to reduce risk to the safety and welfare of the hostages.

Once you're consciously slowing and controlling the pace, you can then move on to the next aspect, which is *engaging* and *explaining*. What do I mean by this? Back in a workplace setting, one of the first things to consider is explaining to the other person how you see yourself in the conversation, effectively your role in it, and then ensuring you address their basic needs. They may have something to tell you, but first they need some control and certainty over the conversation, about what's going to happen.

You also want them to feel empowered, as this may reduce any impulse they may feel to over-comply during the conversation. For example, in a workplace conversation where a line manager is speaking with a colleague, there is a chance that the colleague will be overly compliant if they don't feel empowered in the conversation. They will try to be helpful by going along with what they believe their boss "wants to hear" or is suggesting to them. Some people are frightened of authority figures. So if you're a line manager having one of these conversations, park your ego, role, rank, position, and title. If you are confident in yourself and your own ability, then you can focus your energies on reassuring the other person that you can be trusted and relied on.

Also let's not forget that people who feel vulnerable may also be concerned about presenting themselves in the best possible light and might even pretend to understand when they do not. This can result in them saying what they think you want to hear, rather than what is actually the real issue. To help with the structure of the conversation and before you begin to hear from the other person, it's worth explaining some of the formalities and ground rules that might apply.

- Purpose of the conversation. What are you talking about?

- If you ask a question that the person does not understand or that the person does not know the answer to, the person should say so and you'll clarify.

- If you misunderstand what the person has said or summarize what has been said incorrectly, then the person should point this out too.

- You will point out that the person can ask for a break at any time.

- Mention timing: Is there a limit? Conversations can't go on forever. However, sensitive conversations may need more time, as you are slowing the pace.

- Records: Are you going to make any?

- Are confidentiality agreements required? Who are you going to tell about this conversation?

Once you've established some ground rules, you then need to be thinking about maintaining and building rapport with the other person. The aim is to enable the other person to relax, all of which is a continuous process.

Also consider:

In sensitive conversations, assessing the other person's emotional state and mood, as well as your own, is important so you can remain agile in how you communicate. In addition to this, continue demonstrating respect and empathy for the other person throughout the conversation. One way we can do so, particularly if we need to share some important information such as if they're being sacked, disciplined, or looked over for a promotion, is not to sugarcoat the truth.

Saying what needs to be said first is not only faster, but also kinder. Share what you need to share before you provide the context, background, or rationale for the decision. Leaders sometimes sandwich bad news between bits of positivity. All the while, the other person is wondering why on earth they're having the conversation in the first place.

This is not a green light for rudeness or brutal honesty, but so that the person leaves the conversation feeling genuinely respected and cared for. Whenever you need to have such a conversation, if you work on the basis that everyone else within the organization is listening in, how would you come across? Would they acknowledge that what you're saying and how you're saying it is being done clearly, directly, and fully respecting and empathizing with how the information is being received by the other person?

Particularly in sensitive conversations, be aware of any cognitive biases showing up that you or others may have. We all suffer from them, so it's more a case of being aware and acknowledging them so they don't unfairly impact the conversation. These can range from everything from overconfidence to your values, political beliefs, or the "rules" you have about what you believe should happen in certain circumstances.

If the purpose of the conversation is to elicit information from somebody, once rapport has been established and everyone is settled, ask for a "free narrative account." This does not involve probing and asking detailed questions. Every effort at this stage is directed toward obtaining information from the person that comes spontaneously and is uncontaminated by you asking lots of questions.

Effective prompts to use in these circumstances include: "Tell me about . . . ," "Describe . . ." or "Explain . . ." What is then likely to happen is that the person will probably dump a lot of information on you. They may even recall events in a nonchronological order and flit from one part of the story to another.

Many of their reasons for doing so are perfectly innocent in their nature. They could be genuine mistakes stemming from a memory encoding or recall failure, or even subconscious contamination of their memory. Stress and their frame of reference can affect memory recall. You will need to gradually clarify what was said and draw out more specifics. In this way, you can help the person gently add texture and layers to their story. How do you do this? You need to ask questions.

A word of caution here. Research has found that vulnerable people or those who feel sensitive, by virtue of their age, cognitive ability, or other perceptions about themselves, usually provide less information in their free narrative accounts than people who don't consider themselves to be vulnerable. Nevertheless, this information may still be accurate. Be mindful that answers provided by vulnerable people could be inaccurate because of inappropriate, leading, or suggestive questioning.

So far, you have planned the conversation, set ground rules by engaging and explaining, addressed some basic needs by giving some control and certainty, built rapport, and allowed the person to give a free narrative account. By now, you probably have a mass of information that will need clarifying and probing.

So now what?

The power of questions

Asking powerful questions enables you to enhance both the quality of your negotiations and, ultimately, the quality of your life. Rudyard Kipling deemed questions starting with these six words, the "six honest serving men." They are: *what, why, when, how, where*, and *who*.

Use them constantly to ensure you have understood correctly. However, to avoid your negotiation sounding like an interrogation, they should be used in conjunction with all of the other techniques described in this book. This is particularly so for the active listening skills, such as minimal encouragers, summarizing what someone has just said or done, and labeling their emotions, all of which demonstrate your understanding of where the other person is at. Using these skills will also make them feel psychologically safe as well as seen, heard, and understood.

If you ever feel like rapport has been lost, your ability to influence or persuade will have disappeared. Therefore, it's crucial to get it back before you carry on with the conversation. After receiving the other person's free narrative account, you now need to probe it. It is helpful for you to tell the person that you'll be asking them some questions based on what they've just told you and invite them to expand on and clarify what they have said.

Open questions

Research and practice shows that the most reliable and detailed answers from people of all ages are secured by using open-ended questions. It is important, therefore, that the questioning phase should begin with open-ended questions and that this type of question should be widely employed throughout the conversation.

Be careful of "why" questions, as they can imply blame or guilt. "Why didn't you tell anyone before?" "Why didn't you run away?"

Replace with "what" and "how" questions, which are less accusatory. "What made you keep this to yourself?" "What prevented you from speaking up?"

Here are some of the benefits of open questions:

- They enable the person to provide an unrestricted response.

- They allow the person to control the flow of information.

- They minimize the risk that you will impose your own view of what happened.

- They can introduce a general topic, which then allows the person considerable freedom in determining what to reply.

Mistakes can still be made with open questions, though. Do not ask open questions and follow up the question immediately with closed questions. "How did you get to work today? Did you drive or walk?" "What did you do last night? Stay in or go out?"

This can demonstrate that you are not really interested in their reply or you think you know the answer already, so are narrowing down their options to save time. If you ask an open question, remain silent and allow the other person time to answer. Take turns in conversation. If I ask you an open question while looking at you, it will be very uncomfortable for both of us if you just stare back at me and say nothing. Another mistake you can make in conversations is asking too many questions.

Closed questions

Closed questions can be appropriate or inappropriate depending on the quality of the information likely to be obtained. Closed or forced-choice questions, which often begin with "did" or "do," usually restrict the other person to either yes or no or limited responses, such as asking your kids, "Did you have a good day at school?," which is usually met with an indifferent "Yeah." Specific closed questions can be appropriate, though, when asked in a suggestive way, like the labeling or paraphrasing techniques, for extension or clarification of something the other person has already said.

For example, a colleague or friend shares with you that they didn't get the job they went for. You might then ask them, "Do you think you did the best you could?" Which will likely generate a variation on "No," "Not really," "Yeah," "I guess so." But use these types of questions too much and the person feels under pressure. It also demonstrates little empathy on your part.

Leading questions

Leading questions are leading by virtue of the very nature of the words used. For example, "I bet that hurt, didn't it?" An example of a leading question that follows what the person has already said to you in the conversation might be "Where did he punch you?" when the person said previously that somebody "hit" them, without using the word "punch." Or, if someone says, "I put more clothes on because I was cold," and your follow-up question is: "What coat did you choose?"

These questions convey your assumptions about what happened, rather than the experiences or facts as they were experienced by the person telling their story. Closed and leading questions give the impression that you are not listening or may be judging or rushing the person to answer, which in turn can demonstrate a lack of empathy.

During this questioning phase, which follows their free narrative account, consider generally commencing with open-ended questions and then, if necessary, to more specific closed questions. Use leading questions only as a last resort.

Questions should:

- Be simple.

- Avoid jargon.

- Avoid abstract words or abstract ideas.

- Be free of your own biases and assumptions.

- Contain only one point per question.

- Avoid being too directive or suggestive.

Now that we've covered questioning, let's elaborate on a technique that is an absolutely crucial part of your active listening toolbox and that can be used in conjunction with asking powerful questions.

Verbal mirroring

What is it about mirroring that is so important and effective? Because it is nonthreatening and very subtle, it's an ideal technique to use during sensitive or difficult conversations. It's a better technique to use than asking questions repeatedly, which can resemble an interview or, even worse, an interrogation, especially if you ask too many consecutive open questions too quickly.

It doesn't involve much effort either, yet can encourage the other person to expand on what they're saying. What's more, you can use this technique in emails and text messages too. So how do you do it?

By repeating the last few words spoken by the other person. For example, the person might say, "I had a stressful journey today and missed my train." You would respond with "Missed your train?" If your tone rises at the end of your statement, it sounds like a question. This will encourage the person to expand on their original statement. The beauty of doing this is that you don't need to think of a question, and you get a lot of information as the person expands on what they said, just by mirroring.

A good time to use this technique is when you're feeling under pressure to respond, as it can demonstrate that you're listening as well as give you thinking time. It's also useful when you are overwhelmed, when someone is shouting at you, or when you are faced with or experiencing intense emotions. Mirroring can help you avoid freezing and gets you out of a tight spot when you don't know what to say because your senses are overwhelmed.

Imagine someone shouting at you in a public place, with people standing all around watching, or someone telling you a story and crying hysterically as they do so. If you can't think of anything to say in these moments, just repeat their last few words to give yourself some space and calm your emotions. This gives you some time to think of something meaningful to ask or say.

Finally, another time to use mirroring is when you want to steer the conversation in a direction you think it should go. This can be important when dealing with people who are in an emotional crisis or during a sensitive conversation because a person may be telling you lots about what is going on for them, but within the detail, there is something that needs to be discussed and explored further.

The truth is that there is often another conversation that probably needs to be had. We call them "hooks," and mirroring is a great way to talk about them without making a huge issue about steering the person to discuss them. It's also a good way to keep them on a topic until you have dealt with it as much as you need to.

Chapter Summary

Negotiating with difficult people requires careful planning and understanding of their needs and motivations. By applying the following key techniques, you will enhance your ability to navigate challenging negotiations successfully.

SEEK TO UNDERSTAND: Consider reframing people you perceive as being "difficult" as "worthy opponents" instead. By using language that fosters respect and understanding, you can elevate the negotiation process. This approach helps prevent ego-driven decision-making and assumptions and enables both parties to find mutually beneficial outcomes.

- Action Step: Before entering a negotiation with a "worthy opponent," engage in active listening to gain a deeper understanding of the other person's point of view as well as their "model of the world" and motivations.

CREATE A PLAN AND MANAGE RISKS: Planning is particularly essential in difficult, sensitive, or emotional negotiations. Consider potential risks and challenges that may arise and develop strategies to mitigate them. This preparation will provide you with clarity and confidence during the negotiation. Risk should also not be viewed as a negative aspect but rather an opportunity to manage and overcome challenges.

- Action Step: Prior to the negotiation, spend a few minutes identifying key issues, risks, considerations, and possible solutions. This brief planning time can significantly enhance your preparedness.

SUCCEEDING IN EMOTIONAL NEGOTIATIONS: Difficult conversations often involve heightened emotions. Recognize the influence of emotions on decision-making and strive to manage them effectively. If necessary, label these emotions effectively to ensure a more productive discussion. Name it to tame it! This will enable you to foster a collaborative and respectful environment to address sensitive topics.

- **Action Step** Engage with the other person's impulsive and emotional System One thinking through empathy to influence their logical, decision-making System Two. By also empathizing with and acknowledging their perspective and motivations, you'll earn the right to begin influencing their decision-making process positively.

MEETING PRIMAL NEEDS: Understand that "worthy opponents" may have unspoken needs that must be met before successful negotiation can occur. These needs may include a sense of safety, control, or significance.

- **Action Step:** During the negotiation, focus on identifying and addressing the underlying primal needs of the other person. Find ways to fulfill these needs, fostering a more constructive and productive discussion.

IMPROVE YOUR QUESTIONING SKILLS: The quality of your questions plays a crucial role in the negotiation process. Thoughtful and strategic questions can lead to better outcomes.

- **Action Step:** Enhance your questioning skills by asking better questions. Focus on generating insightful inquiries that promote understanding and constructive dialogue.

By applying these key techniques and taking the suggested action steps, you can improve your ability to negotiate successfully with difficult people. Remember to prioritize understanding, plan effectively, manage risks, and navigate emotional aspects of the negotiation process.

Key Takeaways

1. Meeting your basic needs and theirs will lead to a successful negotiation.

2. By first focusing on the other person's impulsive and emotional System One aspect of the brain through empathy, you can then influence their more logical, decision-making System Two.

3. Time spent planning for difficult conversations is seldom wasted.

4. The quality of your questions dictates the quality of your life. So ask better questions, particularly in difficult negotiations.

Your Five-Step Action Plan for Lifelong Negotiation Success

L *ife is a negotiation.* As we discovered at the very beginning of this book, every single day you are engaging in this activity, even if you don't see yourself as a "negotiator." After all, isn't negotiation just one person communicating with another to influence or persuade them to think, feel, or act in a certain way? This applies whether you are talking with a colleague, family member, or client. Remember, words matter, and being able to negotiate and communicate effectively is one of the most important skills you can ever learn.

In this book, you've learned some powerful negotiation principles, strategies, tools, and techniques, supported by real-life case studies. But knowledge by itself is not enough. The key is to take this knowledge and turn it into meaningful and consistent action and become the best negotiator you can be.

Now is your time to put these new skills to the test. We seem to live in a world more divided than ever, from politics, race, and gender to climate and sexuality. The pragmatic diplomacy of the center ground has given way to tribal extremes, with both sides extolling the virtues of their argument, which they believe will make things better as long as everyone fully subscribes to their mantra and creed. You are either with us or against us. There has never been a more pressing need for you to improve your negotiation and leadership skills to help guide not only yourself, but also your people, through these challenging times.

To simplify everything we've covered, let's look at the five steps you can take to create a simple, quick action plan to make yourself a world-class communicator and win every negotiation.

Step 1: Commit to mastering emotional self-regulation

As we've highlighted throughout this book, at some point in your life, it is highly likely that you will experience extreme stress of one sort or another. This may be the death of a loved one, a major health scare, a sudden job loss, or financial difficulty. On a lesser scale, you will undoubtedly encounter communication challenges, whether in your personal relationships or involving a significant business negotiation.

Realistically, and despite your best efforts, you're unlikely to prevent any of these from occurring. Regardless of the level of stress you experience, it will threaten to trigger negative and disempowering emotions within you.

What can you do then to master emotional self-regulation, so you're not buffeted by the winds of crisis and conflict?

The three key techniques of harnessing your Red Center, taking control of your internal emotional state, and developing your emotional intelligence are crucial to developing a powerful mindset, one capable of communicating and negotiating effectively, regardless of the circumstances.

We start by remembering that a Red Center is not just a physical location for a kidnap negotiation. It's something within you that enables you to park the dark side of your ego and strip back the fear and conditioning that have been hardwired over years and now obstruct your innate human ability to step up and thrive in the face of adversity. Only by doing this will you overcome challenges and achieve your full potential.

First, tune in to your body and develop your awareness and acknowledgment of powerful emotions when they arise and jolt you. When they do, pause, breathe, and learn to be comfortable with being uncomfortable, rather than turning away and avoiding them. Turn toward the frustration, pain, disappointment, anger, or whatever powerful emotion shows up. Then, to avoid being emotionally hijacked once you've accepted the emotion, by all means "feel the feeling," but it's crucial to "drop the story." Don't play the victim. It serves no one. Least of all you. As the ancient Stoic philosopher Epictetus puts it, "It is not events that disturb people; it is their judgments concerning them."

This is not about suppressing emotions, denying your experience, or condoning or acquiescing to injustice or abuse. It's more a case of empowering yourself to create a new state that will in turn help you frame a story or belief in a way that will help you overcome and achieve against all odds, rather than shrink away and self-sabotage. Use emotional self-regulation to focus more on the solutions, rather than the problems.

An example of this might be reading a social media post that conflicts with your values or beliefs, or hearing a colleague tell a joke at your expense, or getting a flat tire on the way home, or a business deal falls apart and the lucrative contract doesn't get signed. What distinguishes us from other animals is what makes us human; namely, the ability to choose.

Viktor Frankl, the Auschwitz survivor and psychotherapist, echoed these sentiments when he said: "Between stimulus and response there is a space. In that space is our power to choose our response. In our response lies our growth and our freedom." You get to choose what you focus on, what it means, and, ultimately, what you're going to do because of that meaning. So choose wisely.

One way to help yourself with this is by improving your emotional intelligence and sensory acuity so you can tune in to the real and often unspoken emotions of every person you communicate with, while also being conscious of your own. This level of self-awareness enhances your ability to evaluate yourself and understand how your behavior is being perceived by others. It also increases the ease with which you can make yourself work with minimal pressure from them.

Developing an empathetic awareness can be made more difficult, however, if you are unable to remain focused on one thing for any length of time. So choose what you focus on and then focus on what you choose. You'll also teach your self-regulation muscles to respond appropriately, rather than merely reacting in a knee-jerk fashion. From here, you can harness the power of your very own Red Center to develop the psychological and emotional resilience that no matter how many "worthy opponents" you come across, you will take them in your stride and create something even greater as a result.

Step 2: Time spent in preparation is seldom wasted

Once you've established your winning mindset and psychology, you need to move on to the next phase of becoming a world-class communicator. Success in any field, but particularly negotiation, requires planning and preparation. Not just as a one-off, but all the time, constantly striving toward excellence. Because if you don't and you find yourself under pressure in a crisis or conflict situation, your ability to communicate will fall to your highest level of preparation.

What is more, Murphy's Law says that no matter what you do to prepare, other people will often fail to do what you expect of them and that therefore things are unlikely to go according to plan. This is why the more realistic and challenging the preparation you put yourself and your teams through to withstand whatever occurs, the greater your chances of negotiation success.

Regardless of the circumstances, by following a three-step checklist each time—managing your state, utilizing your Red Center, and visualizing success ahead of time, having already considered the worst-case scenario or Bunch of Fives—you'll be able to take things in your stride and retain that invaluable calmness at the center of the storm, when powerful emotions threaten to sweep you off your feet.

Consistent negotiation success is achieved because of a team of people able to play to their strengths. While they may be able to perform many roles, only one or two of these roles will be in alignment with their true nature and personality. If it really is just you by yourself, then remember you can still split the communication from the decision-making, a vital tactic if you want to avoid conceding too much. When in doubt, always remember the adage: negotiators negotiate; commanders command.

Surrounding yourself with a first-class team helps you succeed in negotiating. It also affords you the opportunity to schedule time for yourself during the day to recharge and prevent burnout. One way of supporting yourself with this is by creating your own morning and evening routines. For a lot of people operating in high-stakes environments, taking the time alone to focus quietly on the day that lies ahead or to reflect on it at the end is important, as it can help place things in perspective. It also calms and grounds the nervous system, which is essential if you want to be an effective negotiator.

Another option is to combine this with regular exercise, away from the distraction of laptops, mobile phones, and other devices. This enables you to stay engaged in whatever form of communication you're in with high levels of energy and focus.

Despite your best efforts of planning and prevention, though, sometimes things will still threaten to knock you off course. When this happens, you can activate your Immediate Action drill by:

1. **Interrupting the pattern** by shifting your focus, language, and body to change your state.

2. **Refusing to allow** a negative thought or feeling to take hold for more than ninety seconds, by which time the naturally occurring stress chemicals will have dissipated.

3. **Asking empowering questions** of yourself, such as: "What else could this mean?," "Where is the gift in this situation?," "What is the opportunity or learning for me?," "What am I not seeing here?," "How can this enable me to grow?"

Step 3: Increase your knowledge of negotiation psychology to influence and persuade anyone

So, you've harnessed your Red Center, increased your mastery of emotional self-regulation, and discovered the power of being able to remain balanced, calm, and laser-focused on the communication at hand. Not only that, but you've got your Immediate Action drill in your back pocket ready to pull out and use if required. Finally, you've identified and established your own version of a CMT that will provide you with invaluable support to help you succeed in negotiations over the long term. So what's next?

It's time for action. This book is ultimately about you taking determined and focused action in order to achieve meaningful results in all aspects of your communication. It's no good just reading about something and increasing your knowledge on a topic, however interesting it may be. You have to be able to physically apply it in the real world and reap the benefits.

You now know that the emotions you feel are made up of your varied life experiences, bodily sensations in any given moment, and the words and actions of the people you're with, rather than being driven by a so-called reptilian brain. Nor is this part of your brain constantly threatening to overpower your ability to have calm, rational thought.

Remember, you are not a passive receiver of sensory input but rather an active constructor of your emotions. This means that you get to choose in every single second what you focus on, interpret what it means, and then decide what you are going to do. You are a feeling creature that thinks, rather than a thinking creature that feels.

This is particularly important when you get stressed or triggered and your sympathetic nervous system takes a beating. Avoid leaving this unchecked for too long, otherwise it could lead to chronic inflammation and illness.

Focusing on what caused it in the first place allows you to choose whether to continue repeating your patterns of disempowering language, thoughts, and behaviors. In any case, feel free to surf that cortisol wave for ninety seconds, utilizing powerful breathing techniques to calm you, after which you can choose whether to keep feeding that particular emotion (your "story") or select another, more helpful approach.

By now, you've also made friends with the four characters of your brain, so it's time to determine which character is more dominant and which ones you need to give more attention to increase your negotiation mastery. While you won't always need to script what you want to say, like in a kidnap negotiation, taking a few moments beforehand will allow you to communicate a message that will be clear, impactful, and, ultimately, achieve your outcome, which is to influence or persuade the other person. Remember, clarity is power.

To take your ability to influence and persuade to the next level, learn to listen more. Yes, you heard that right. One of the most powerful Jedi-mind tricks is to do just that: a deep, level-five form of listening that provides you with an understanding of how the other person sees the world around them. This knowledge will in turn show you how to build meaningful rapport and best serve them with what they need and want.

Engaging at this level of listening, however demanding it can be, also helps to diffuse the unhealthy aspects of your ego that might otherwise get in the way of you succeeding. This is why it's important to achieve a solid foundation for positive communication and relationships with others. Ask yourself better questions about your intention in the negotiation itself. Ask whether you're being honest in your communications, or are you just trying to manipulate the other person? Are you really being empathetic and seeing things from their perspective, or just concentrating on your own point of view?

To get to level-five listening and bring about the behavior change you're seeking, incorporate the active listening techniques of MOREPIES, such as paraphrasing and emotional labeling, in all of your communications. Remember that it's not a rigid, checklist system, but a toolkit to be used appropriately depending on the person and context.

Step 4: Mistakes are a fact of life; it's your response to them that counts

People frequently make mistakes when communicating with others, none more so than when negotiating. Communication mistakes are particularly common when emotions are running high, and they can obstruct true empathetic listening, regardless of how they're made. Most of us can think of times when we've been on the receiving end of poor communication.

The first mistake usually takes the form of personal barriers, such as bragging or offering unsolicited advice about what should be done; the rush to problem-solve is widespread. The second mistake is the blocks within your organization that impede effective communication. They are usually found in the guise of systems, processes, or the pervading culture. If you can identify both your personal barriers and the organizational blocks that you're able to overcome, you'll be miles head of the next person.

You can also avoid falling into the same trap yourself, by learning to develop an awareness of your habitual, automatic language patterns, thought processes, and behaviors. Learn how they can sneak up on you and rule the show. As a leader, you must go first by taking full responsibility for these, rather than blaming others. Avoid these mistakes in the first place by moving through each part of the Communication Sequence in turn, spending sufficient time at each stage before moving on to the next:

Active listening

Empathy

Rapport

Trust-based influence

Behavior change

Remember, this isn't meant to be a hard-and-fast rule or a strict process to slavishly follow. Consider it more as a handrail that can guide you along the negotiation path. Despite your best efforts to prevent or overcome communication blocks or barriers, not all negotiations go as well as you'd like them to, with conflict or uncertainty sometimes lingering like a bad smell.

Resistance isn't always futile. Often, it's important to establish and maintain boundaries as well as red lines about what's important to you. This applies in your personal life just as much as it does in a kidnap negotiation. Rapport can still be maintained during times of heated conflict. Avoid being so fixated on these boundaries and red lines that you inadvertently overlook an even better outcome than the original one.

Faced with such a situation, practice focusing on the four areas of nonviolent communication: observe without judgment what is happening in the situation; state how you feel when you observe this behavior; articulate your needs connected with that feeling; and, finally, make a specific request of what you want to happen.

Finally, regularly practice draining the swamp of all resistance. This is all the criticism, negativity, and perceptions other people may have about you, your latest idea or business proposal, however unjustified they may be. Most people make the mistake of ignoring these barriers, hoping they'll just disappear. But like the proverbial elephant in the room, unless you raise and address them from the outset by laying them out on the table before the other side do, they'll remain unspoken and prevent people from engaging with you as fully as they might do otherwise.

Step 5: Seek out worthy opponents; they'll turn you into a negotiation superstar

Not all conversations are easy. Every kidnapping case I worked on included people who you could describe as difficult. They ranged from the kidnappers themselves to the client, the hostage's family, the media, government officials, and a whole host of other stakeholders.

It is a fact of life that you will encounter many people through your work life or at home that you might class as difficult. Some may even think the same of you. What's your best strategy to deal with them and have effective conversations and negotiations?

Follow the advice of the great Roman emperor and Stoic philosopher Marcus Aurelius, who regularly reminded himself when he encountered such people: "The best revenge is not to be like that." When you find yourself stuck in an emotional and stressful conversation, consider that you most likely have no idea what this person has been through. One of the first steps you should take is to identify both your emotional state and theirs. Then you can determine whether you need to manage that before engaging in the negotiation in earnest.

Another step we might consider is using better language and seeing them as "worthy opponents," rather than "difficult." Reframing them in this way will help you understand what truly motivates and drives them. You will then have a "map of their world" that will give insight into whether their basic human needs for safety, control, and recognition are being met. From this new vantage point, you have far more room to negotiate than if you were to see them merely as difficult. This approach also prevents you from being driven purely by your ego, particularly if it requires either side to "save face" by backing down over some contentious aspect of a deal.

It's also vital to understand the difference between their *needs* versus their *wants*. People rarely express their needs outright. They might hint at them, but they'll rarely share them with you. If you take your time and work through the Communication Sequence as described earlier in the book, however, you will uncover them. Once you've done this, you can prioritize meeting their needs rather than getting distracted by their wants. This is particularly useful when you are unable or unwilling to give them what they want. For example, a hostage-taker may want a getaway car. He's never going to be allowed one, but if the negotiator can determine that his real need is actually for safety or certainty, it might be possible to reassure him that, if he were to surrender, he will be safe and no harm will come to him.

Apart from asking great questions, remember that human beings don't negotiate or make decisions rationally or objectively, so consider how you can use your new improved empathy and language abilities to influence the other person's System One thinking—their impulsive, intuitive, and emotional aspects. People can't truly listen when they are in this zone and in a high emotional state. As you now know, this will directly impact what happens in their System Two thinking; i.e., their slow, deliberate, and logical thinking and behavior. This is where we want to move people to when having these types of challenging conversations.

Difficult, sensitive, or emotional conversations usually benefit from some form of planning beforehand. You don't necessarily have to spend a long time doing this; just consider your desired outcomes and why they are important. Once you've established those key aspects, you can then focus on which approach will work best, such as asking powerful, open questions that enable you first to understand where the other person is coming from, and why, before you even begin to think about wanting them to understand your position.

Undertaking some planning before you engage with your "worthy opponent" is likely to help you identify the level of risk involved. Once you've determined this, now what? One avenue might be for you to use the risk management guidelines of: tolerate, treat, terminate, or transfer the risk.

A Final Word

D espite what you may have previously been led to believe, practice doesn't make perfect. It makes permanent. Practice these techniques in those conversations that have a low risk of fallout if they don't go as well as you'd like them to, such as getting the kids ready for school or having a minor conversation in the workplace. As the world's number-one life and business strategist Tony Robbins says: "Repetition is the mother of all skill." Start small. Avoid seeking out huge and immediate paradigm shifts in your thoughts, words, and behavior or in those of others. You've got a lifetime of communication hiccups to undo.

This is about making small steps, consistently applied, that will ultimately lead to long-term and sustainable success. Every single day is awash with opportunities for you to communicate either positively or negatively. If you can't always do so positively, at least be neutral rather than negative in your approach. This can apply to the multimillion-dollar business deal as easily as it can to the poorly written email or social media post you send when you're tired or in a bad mood or have been "triggered." The subsequent effect on others is contagious.

Equally, small acts of generosity or kindness in how you communicate, however challenging or stressful the circumstances, are equally as contagious, encouraging the recipients to pay it forward and do the same.

As highlighted right at the very start of this book, there is a pressing need to turn and face the conflict and challenges in the world today, seeking mutual areas of inclusion rather than division. One way we can do this is by using the negotiation and leadership skills and techniques found through-out this book. They will enable you to have better conversations with others and find that courageous, curious, and caring voice inside of you. This is your path to success in any communication situation you find yourself in. It is ultimately only in this way that we will bring order out of chaos.

Appendix A

Time spent in preparation is seldom wasted. This is particularly so when engaging in challenging, difficult, or complex negotiations. One way to prepare is to write a "position paper." This short document ideally fits onto one side of a piece of letter-size paper, two at the maximum. Its purpose is to get you laser-focused on the key aspects of the negotiation and help you to avoid any miscommunication or assumptions.

Your position paper can also help you capture the key outcomes of each meeting or phone call in the negotiation and identify the reason why each outcome is important.

Crucially, this document is not meant to be a verbatim script to be followed to the letter. See it more as a handrail; it's there if you need it, rather than a set of rules that must be adhered to at all costs. That way, you'll be able to retain your agility, rather than be hemmed into a position you can't maneuver out of.

A position paper is also great if you have to brief senior leaders in an organization when important decisions have to be made. It's been used highly successfully in corporate settings, just as much as it has in fraught kidnap negotiations in the Middle East, Latin America, and elsewhere.

Position paper

Position paper as at [insert date]

_____

_____

Background (to the circumstances you find yourself in)

_____

_____

Situation (the current position)

_____

_____

Assessment (risks, likelihood, probability, consequences, mitigation)

_____

_____

Options (include outcomes along with pros and cons for each option)

_____

_____

Summary (of above)

_____

_____

Recommendations and next steps (with rationale and time frame)

_____

_____

Appendix B

Negotiation prompt

The following prompt can be used in all types of negotiation, whether you are at home or in the boardroom. Have a copy of it to hand in your journal, laptop bag, or even on a sticky note that you can refer to just before you walk into a crucial client meeting or have that important conversation with your kids.

Key considerations

- Slow is smooth; smooth is fast.

- Don't rush to problem-solve.

- Seek first to understand, before being understood.

- Convey zero judgment with the tone of voice or words you use.

- We all just want to feel safe, seen, heard, and understood.

Active listening skills

M   Minimal encouragers (Mmm . . . , Uh-huh . . . , I see . . . , Yeah . . .)

O   Open-ended questions (What . . . ?, How . . . ?, Tell me about . . .)

R   Reflecting/mirroring (repeat their last two or three key words)

E   Effective pauses (encourages them to keep talking)

P   Paraphrasing (reflecting back your understanding of what the other person said in your own words)

I   "I" Message (I feel x when you y because z)

E   Emotional labeling (It looks like . . . , It seems like . . . , It feels like . . . , It sounds like . . .)

S   Summarizing (use their words to demonstrate understanding)

Acknowledgments

While this book may have been the dream of one person and has only my name on the cover, it required an outstanding team to make it a reality. I've been blessed to have found such a team and couldn't have asked for a more capable, enthusiastic, and supportive bunch of people. Thanks once again to my agent, Ben Clark at the Soho Agency, who saw the spark and had the vision. Also to Abby Koons and the other Ben (KZ) at Park and Fine who worked their magic across the pond. Finally to my editor Scott Berinato and the rest of the team at HBR who believed in this book from the outset. Thank you all.

And then there is the finest team of crisis response consultants I could ever learn from. Particular thanks go to GA, for taking a chance on me; to TL, for providing unfailing support and top cover; it was an honor, sir. MR, thank you for your wise counsel and friendship. You need to work on your jokes, though. KW planting the seed to do this work in the first place. DO, MB, SB, JY, RA, JS, and BL were great "Red Center" mentors who taught me a lot.

Last, but by no means least, to all the kidnap victims, their families, and colleagues, as well as those struggling in a crisis, thank you for allowing me into your world to help you as best I could when the stakes couldn't get any higher.

Chapter References

Chapter One: Mastering a Negotiator's Mindset

Henley, W. E. (1889). *A Book of Verses.* (New York. hdl:2027/hvd.hwk9sr)

"The 5 Aspects of Emotional Intelligence and Why They Matter." Awâto website. February 1, 2018. https://awato.co/5-aspects-emotional-intelligence-matter/.

Huberman, A. "Master Your Emotions." YouTube video, 00:21:08. "Architecture of a Feeling." https://hubermanlab.com/the-science-of-emotions-relationships/.

Richardson, A. "Mental Practice: A Review and Discussion, Part 1." *Research Quarterly. American Association for Health, Physical Education and Recreation* 38, no. 1 (1967): 95–107.

Kearns, D. W., and J. Crossman. "Effects of a Cognitive Intervention Package on the Free-Throw Performance of Varsity Basketball Players During Practice and Competition." Supplement, *Perceptual and Motor Skills* 75, no. 3 (1992): 1243–1253.

Frankl, V. *Man's Search for Meaning.* Part 1, translated by Ilse Lasch. Boston: Beacon Press, 2006. First published 1946.

Salovey, P., and J. D. Mayer. "Emotional Intelligence." *Imagination, Cognition and Personality* 9 (1990): 185–211.

Kabat-Zinn, J. *Full Catastrophe Living.* London: Little, Brown, 2013.

Bruch, H., and S. Ghoshal. "Beware the Busy Manager." *Harvard Business Review,* February 2002. https://hbr.org/2002/02/beware-the-busy-manager.

Peters, S. *The Chimp Paradox: The Mind Management Program to Help You Achieve Success, Confidence, and Happiness.* London: Random House, 2012.

Coyle, D. *The Culture Code: The Secrets of Highly Successful Groups.* London: Random House, 2018.

Chapter Two: Preparing to Win Every Negotiation

Kotler, S. *The Rise of Superman: Decoding the Science of Ultimate Human Performance.* London: Quercus, 2014.

Kotler, S. "Create a Work Environment That Fosters Flow." *Harvard Business Review,* October 2019. https://hbr.org/2014/05/create-a-work-environment-that-fosters-flow.

Csikszentmihalyi, M. *Flow: The Psychology of Optimal Experience*. New York: Harper & Rowe, 1990.

Collins, J. *Good to Great: Why Some Companies Make the Leap and Others Don't*. London: Random House, 2001.

Zenko, M. *Red Team: How to Succeed by Thinking Like the Enemy*. New York: Perseus Books Group, 2015.

2nd public hearing of the National Commission on Terrorist Attacks upon the United States. May 22, 2003. Statement of Bogdan Dzakovic. https://www.9 -11commission.gov/hearings/hearing2/witness_dzakovic.htm.

Chapter Three: Practical Psychology to Influence Any Negotiation

Beck, A. T. *Cognitive Therapy and the Emotional Disorders*. New York: Penguin, 1976.

MacLean, P. D. *The Triune Brain in Evolution: Role in Paleocerebral Functions*. New York: Plenum Press, 1990.

McKay, S. "Rethinking the Reptilian Brain." Dr. Sarah McKay website (blog). June 24, 2020. https://drsarahmckay.com/rethinking-the-reptilian-brain/.

Feldman Barrett, L. *How Emotions Are Made: The Secret Life of the Brain*. London: Macmillan, 2017.

Bolte Taylor, J. *Whole Brain Living: The Anatomy of Choice and the Four Characters That Drive Our Life*. London: Hay House UK, 2021.

Bolte Taylor, J. "My Stroke of Insight." TED Talks. 2008. https://www.ted.com /talks/jill_bolte_taylor_my_stroke_of_insight.

Langley, J. *The Autonomic Nervous System Part 1*. Cambridge: W. Heffer, 1921.

Frankl, V. *Man's Search for Meaning*. Part 1 translated by Ilse Lasch. Boston: Beacon Press, 2006. First published 1946.

Mehrabian, A. *Nonverbal Communication*. Piscataway, NJ: Aldine Transaction, 1972.

Hemingway, E. *Across the River and into the Trees*. New York: C. Scribner's Sons, 1950.

Kotler, S. *The Rise of Superman: Decoding the Science of Ultimate Human Performance*. London: Quercus, 2014.

Rogers, C. R., and R. E. Farson. *Active Listening*. Chicago: Industrial Relations Center of the University of Chicago, 1957.

Mnookin, R. H., S. R. Peppet, and A. S. Tulumello. *Beyond Winning: Negotiating to Create Value in Deals and Disputes*. Cambridge, MA: Belknap Press of Harvard University Press, 2000.

Spencer, H. *The Principles of Biology*. London: Williams and Norgate, 1864.

Darwin, C. *The Descent of Man, and Selection in Relation to Sex*. New York: D. Appleton & Co., 1871.

Allison, E., and L. Allison. *Rapport: The Four Ways to Read People*. London: Vermilion, 2020.

Chapter Four: Avoiding Common Negotiation Mistakes

Rosenberg, M. B. *Nonviolent Communication: A Language of Life*. Encinitas, CA: Puddle Dancer Press, 2015.

Chapter Five: Negotiating with Difficult People

Rumi. "Out Beyond Ideas of Wrongdoing and Rightdoing." *The Essential Rumi*. Translated from Persian by C. Barks. New York: Harper Collins, 1995.

Fisher, R., and W. Ury. *Getting to Yes: Negotiating Agreement Without Giving In*. Boston: Houghton Mifflin, 1981.

Kahneman, D. *Thinking, Fast and Slow*. London: Penguin, 2011.

Feldman Barrett, L. *Seven and a Half Lessons About the Brain*. London: Picador, 2020.

Vrij, A., L. Hope, and R. P. Fisher. "Eliciting Reliable Information in Investigative Interviews." *Policy Insights from the Behavioral and Brain Sciences* 1, no. 1 (2014): 129–136. https://doi.org/10.1177/2372732214548592.

Kipling, R. "The Elephant's Child." *Just So Stories*. London: Macmillan, 1902.

Albudaiwi, D. "Survey: Open-Ended Questions." In *The Sage Encyclopedia of Communication Research Methods*, ed. M. Allen, 1716–1717. Thousand Oaks, CA: SAGE Publications, 2017. https://dx.doi.org/10.4135/9781483381411.n608.

Marcus Aurelius. *Meditations*, Book VI, (6), (c. 161–180 AD).

Epictetus. *Discourses and Selected Writings*. London: Penguin Classics, 2008.

Mnookin, R. H. *Bargaining with the Devil: When to Negotiate, When to Fight*. New York: Simon & Schuster, 2011.

Maslow, A. H. "A Theory of Human Motivation." *Psychological Review* 50, no. 4 (1943): 370–396.

Robbins, A. *Awaken the Giant Within*. London: Simon & Schuster, 1992.

Your Five-Step Action Plan for Lifelong Negotiation Success

Frankl, V. *Man's Search for Meaning*. Part 1, translated by Ilse Lasch. Boston: Beacon Press, 2006. First published 1946.

Further Reading

Barker, E. *Barking Up the Wrong Tree: The Surprising Science Behind Why Everything You Know About Success Is (Mostly) Wrong.* New York: Harper Collins, 2017.

Cialdini, R. B. *Influence: The Psychology of Persuasion,* rev. ed. New York: Harper Business, 2006.

Dutton, K., and A. McNab. *The Good Psychopath's Guide to Success.* London: Bantam Press, 2014.

Dweck, C. *Mindset: Changing the Way You Think to Fulfil Your Potential,* rev. ed. London: Robinson, 2017.

Goleman, D. *Emotional Intelligence: Why It Can Matter More Than IQ.* London: Bloomsbury, 1996.

Hanson, R. *Resilient: Find Your Inner Strength.* London: Rider, 2018.

Holiday, R. *Stillness Is the Key: An Ancient Strategy for Modern Life.* London: Profile Books, 2019.

Kohlrieser, G. *Hostage at the Table: How Leaders Can Overcome Conflict, Influence Others, and Raise Performance.* San Francisco: Jossey-Bass, 2006.

Korb, A. *The Upward Spiral. Using Neuroscience to Reverse the Course of Depression One Small Change at a Time.* Oakland, CA: New Harbinger Publications, 2015.

Lafrance, A., and A. Miller. *What to Say to Kids When Nothing Seems to Work: A Practical Guide for Parents and Caregivers.* New York: Routledge, 2020.

Lopez, B. *The Negotiator: My Life at the Heart of the Hostage Trade.* London: Sphere, 2011.

Maté, G., and D. Maté. *The Myth of Normal: Trauma, Illness and Healing in a Toxic Culture.* London: Vermilion, 2022.

McMains, M. J., W. C. Mullins, and A. T. Young. *Crisis Negotiations: Managing Critical Incidents and Hostage Situations in Law Enforcement and Corrections,* 6th ed. New York: Routledge, 2021.

Middleton, A. *Zero Negativity: The Power of Positive Thinking.* London: Harper Collins, 2020.

Noesner, G. *Stalling for Time: My Life as an FBI Hostage Negotiator.* New York: Random House, 2018.

Powell, J. *Talking to Terrorists: How to End Armed Conflicts*. London: Bodley Head, 2014.

Shortland, A. *Kidnap: Inside the Ransom Business*. Oxford: Oxford University Press, 2019.

Stone, D., B. Patton, and S. Heen. *Difficult Conversations: How to Discuss What Matters Most*, rev. ed. New York: Penguin, 2010.

Voss, C., and T. Raz. *Never Split the Difference: Negotiating as If Your Life Depended on It*. London: Random House Business, 2016.

Waite, T. *Taken on Trust: An Autobiography*. London: Hodder & Stoughton, 1993.

Walker, M. *Why We Sleep: The New Science of Sleep and Dreams*. London: Penguin, 2018.

Index

About the Author

SCOTT WALKER is one of the world's most experienced kidnap-for-ransom negotiators and a former UN counterterrorism adviser. He is also a highly compelling and in-demand keynote speaker.

He spent sixteen years as a Scotland Yard detective engaged in counterterrorism and covert operations before leaving in 2015 to support organizations, government departments, and individuals in negotiating the release of hostages all over the world. His experience has helped him resolve over three hundred cases and other similar crises, such as extortion and piracy, including in Latin America, the Middle East, Africa, and the Asia-Pacific region.

He has also deployed overseas as part of a military intelligence interrogation team to interdict and question High-Value Targets.

Walker now spends his time working with leaders at all levels of an organization to enhance their resilience, emotional intelligence, and communication skills.

Order out of Chaos is his first book and was an immediate UK *Sunday Times* bestseller.

He lives in London with his family.